COMANCHES
AND
MENNONITES
ON THE
OKLAHOMA PLAINS

A.J. and Magdalena Becker
and the Post Oak Mission

Perspectives on Mennonite Life and Thought is a series jointly published between Kindred Productions, the Historical Commission of the General Conference of Mennonite Brethren Churches and the Center for Mennonite Brethren Studies of Winnipeg, Manitoba, Fresno, California, and Hillsboro, Kansas.*

*Volumes 1-4 were published by the Center for Mennonite Brethren Studies (Fresno)

COMANCHES AND MENNONITES ON THE OKLAHOMA PLAINS

A.J. and Magdalena Becker and the Post Oak Mission

MARVIN E. KROEKER

WINNIPEG, MB CANADA — KINDRED PRODUCTIONS — HILLSBORO, KS USA

COMANCHES AND MENNONITES
ON THE OKLAHOMA PLAINS
A.J. and Magdalena Becker and the Post Oak Mission

Canadian Cataloguing in Publication Data
Kroeker, Marvin E., 1928-
Comanches and Mennonites on the Oklahoma plains
(Perspectives on Mennonite life and thought : 12)
Includes bibliographical references and index.
ISBN: 0-921788-42-8

1. Becker, Abraham J.   2. Becker, Magdalena
3. Post Oak Mission – History.   4. Mennonite
Brethren Church of North America – Missions –
Oklahoma.   5. Comanche Indians – Missions – Oklahoma –
History.   6. Missionaries – Oklahoma – Biography.
I. Title.   II. Series.

BX814.B434K76 1997 289.7'092'2766 C97-920057-1

Published simultaneously by Kindred Productions, Winnipeg MB R2L 2E5 and Kindred Productions, Hillsboro KS 67063

Cover Photo: Dedication of Quanah Parker monument, May 4, 1930.
Seated left to right: Lewis Ware, Jim Nance, Baldwin Parker, Lt. Col. Leslie McNain, Harry Stroud. Standing on right: Rev. and Mrs. Becker, Herman Asenap, and To-pay

Cover design by Makus Design, Winnipeg MB

Book Design by Makus Design, Winnipeg MB

Printed in Canada by The Christian Press, Winnipeg

International Standard Book Number: 0-921788-42-8

Dedicated
To my grandchildren

Contents

Foreword

The Mennonite Brethren of the United States and Canada have had a commitment to evangelism out of all proportion to their numbers, being active in both home and foreign missions. The subject of this fine study, the Post Oak Mission of the Comanches, has received relatively little historical attention from the denomination, in contrast to that accorded its work in more exotic areas such as Africa and China.

Marvin Kroeker, who was born and reared in a Mennonite Brethren community in western Oklahoma that was supportive of Post Oak Mission, earned a Ph.D. in History from the University of Oklahoma, and has several publications to his credit. Dr. Kroeker's treatment of his subject is scholarly and objective, despite his obvious and understandable admiration for the central figures in his account, Abraham J. and Magdalena Becker.

The Beckers had those exemplary qualities common to most individuals who became missionaries. They were dedicated to sharing with other peoples the articles of their faith and the benefits of their society, even at the expense of their own creature comforts. The Beckers suffered all the hardships that were the lot of frontier settlers, without the prospect of seeing their labor rewarded with a homestead carved from the virgin prairie. What they did achieve was the development of the Post Oak Mission into, arguably, the most successful one in western Oklahoma.

The Comanches, formerly nomadic warriors and hunters, were as resistant to the missionary message as any other Indians. But what they discovered in the Beckers was not only a concern for their souls; these missionaries were dedicated to helping the Comanches achieve a more healthy and productive way of life. The Beckers were there to help at all stages, from birth to death. It is not surprising that the Indians grew to recognize that these missionaries were their true friends and had come to make a life among them – and to rest among them when that life ended.

The Beckers were a harmonious and highly effective team. A missionary wife's wholehearted cooperation was essential to his success. What made Magdalena's contribution of more than usual importance to the success of Post Oak Mission was her becoming a half-time field matron in the Indian Service.

Field matrons were expected to visit the homes of Indian families in their districts, instructing the women in everything from health care and housekeeping to garment making. Magdalena traveled hundreds of miles a month, usually by buggy and over unimproved roads. Her obvious concern for those whose homes she visited, and her willingness to work alongside the women so as to teach by example, not only furthered the government's civilization program but quickly swelled the Indian attendance at Post Oak religious services.

Dr. Kroeker provides us a thorough account of the evolution of a highly successful mission among Plains Indians. Not only are the missionaries given their due, but he deals sympathetically with the efforts of the Indians to escape mission status and establish their own independent Mennonite Brethren congregation. That they ultimately accomplished this was conclusive evidence that Post Oak Mission had been a success.

William T. Hagan

Preface

The Mennonite Brethren denomination has a well-earned reputation for being a "missionary church." Despite its small size, it
has sent a remarkably high number of workers to mission fields
around the globe. The first "foreign" mission of the Mennonite Brethren Church of North America was authorized in 1895 and established the following year among the Comanche Indians in Oklahoma Territory. The first missionary appointed to the field was Henry
Kohfeld. After twelve years of devoted but generally unproductive
effort, he was replaced by his young assistant, Abraham J. Becker and
his capable wife Magdalena. They put the mission on a firm foundation and spent the rest of their lives among the Comanches on the
Oklahoma frontier.

Considering their historic identification with missions, it is surprising that so little has been written by the Mennonite Brethren
about this pioneering and long-lasting mission enterprise directed by
the Beckers. Local and regional non-Mennonite historians have shown
more interest in Post Oak Mission and the early missionaries than
have recent Mennonite scholars.

During the first half of this century, writers of Mennonite Brethren history recognized the importance of Post Oak in the development of missions activity. John F. Harms, intimately involved in the
mission's establishment, and John H. Lohrenz both incorporated the
early history of Post Oak into their published works. Furthermore, as
editor of the *Zionsbote*, Harms regularly publicized the activities of
the mission. Mrs. H. T. Esau's 1954 study of Mennonite Brethren
missions also provided readers with valuable factual information about
this first missionary outreach sponsored by the denomination. Thus,
during the early decades of its existence, Mennonite Brethren in the
United States and Canada were generally well-informed about the
"Becker Mission" in Chief Quanah Parker's backyard, and eagerly
supported its development.[1]

Later church historians tended to focus on the larger mission
fields in India, China, and Africa, to the neglect of Post Oak. The
most prolific writer on Mennonite Brethren missions, Gerhard W.
Peters, scarcely noted the effort among the Comanches. John A.
Toews, in his scholarly history of the Mennonite Brethren Church
published in 1975, devoted only one brief paragraph to the Oklahoma mission story. J. B. Toews' *Pilgrimage of Faith* (1993) discussed
the beginnings of Mennonite Brethren missions and the church's early

missionaries at length without mentioning the first official field established by the General Conference. As a result of the scant attention given to Post Oak during the last forty years, this once well-known mission—and the faithful church workers who labored there—have faded into undeserved obscurity.[2]

This book is a narrative account of the life and work of Abraham and Magdalena Hergert Becker among the Comanches in southwestern Oklahoma. Abraham Becker's service as missionary and administrator and Magdalena's career as missionary and field matron in the Indian Service form the centerpiece of the study. The history of the Beckers and the history of Post Oak Mission are closely intertwined. The "foreign" mission period of Post Oak extended from 1895, when the Mennonite Brethren Conference officially authorized the work, to 1959, when the mission became an independent Mennonite Brethren church. In one way or another, Rev. Becker was associated with Post Oak for all but about nine of those years; Magdalena Becker spent thirty-seven years among the Comanches. The scope, nature, and impact of the couple's mission work at Post Oak and the surrounding area are examined. Changes in Comanche culture and life caused by the presence of missionaries, white settlers, Indian Office officials, and government policies are also treated. Two chapters on the post-Becker era are included to round out the Post Oak Mission story. They cover the forced relocation of the mission and historic cemetery, and the steps implemented to create an independent Indian Mennonite Brethren church.

Both written and Comanche oral history were utilized in my research. The spelling and hyphenization of Comanche names posed a problem since spellings often changed over time. Generally I follow the spelling used by Indian descendants today, or the usage of acknowledged authorities.

It is my hope that tracing the saga of this missionary couple will bring proper recognition to them and their associates and successors, and to the faithful Comanche leaders, who together created and nurtured a Native American church that exists to this day. Missionaries are frequently characterized as self-righteous and misguided individuals who destroyed Native American cultures under the guise of Christianity and "civilization." While there are many examples that can be cited to support the generalization, recent scholarship has demonstrated that exceptions are sufficiently notable that it can not be accepted uncritically.[3] A. J. and Magdalena Becker are among the exceptions. They believed that as "new creatures in Christ" the Indians—like all true converts—would change their life styles, but they never insisted they cast off their "Indianness."

My interest in Post Oak Mission and the Comanche Indians began as a young boy when my parents took me along on their trips to visit the mission station. Over the years we also visited some of the camp meetings on the mission compound. I recall the excitement of seeing Indians with their tepees, their jerky drying in the sun, and Chief Quanah Parker's imposing monument in the nearby cemetery. My academic interest in the American Indians was nurtured by an array of outstanding Indian historians at the University of Oklahoma, including Edward E. Dale, Don Berthrong, and A. M. Gibson. At Tabor College, L. J. Franz laid the foundation of historical method and research. This study offered the opportunity to combine my two major research interests, Indians and Mennonites.

This endeavor could not have been completed without the kind assistance of others. I am particularly indebted to Glenn Becker who agreed to share any and all materials and personal information he had on his parents and their work at Post Oak. Without his help and encouragement, and the hospitality of his wife Routh, this project would not have been completed. I cannot overstate the importance of the cooperation and support I received from the Post Oak Comanches. Among the many who shared information were Carleton Hoahwah, Marjorie Kelley, Mary Alice Maddox, Wilfred Niedo, Lizzie Pahcheka, Rhoda Tate, Annie Mae Lonetree, Virgie Kassanavoid, and Forrest Kassanavoid. Research materials and other assistance were provided by Peggy Goertzen and Lois Hiebert, Center for Mennonite Brethren Studies, Hillsboro, Kansas, and Paul Toews and Kevin Enns-Remple, Center for Mennonite Brethren Studies, Fresno, California. William Welge, Director of the Oklahoma Historical Society's Division of Manuscripts and Records, Chester Cowan in the photographic department, and the entire archival staff provided courteous and professional assistance of inestimable value. Ann Cummings of the National Archives and Records Division uncovered some crucial correspondence relating to the establishment of Post Oak Mission. Staff members at the Museum of the Great Plains, Lawton Public Library, Fort Worth Federal Records Center, Western History Collections of the University of Oklahoma, and the library and newspaper division of the Oklahoma Historical Society also provided helpful assistance. William T. Hagan and Bob Blackburn read an earlier draft of this manuscript and made helpful suggestions to improve the work. The maps were compiled with the assistance of Victor Murray and a class directed by James Lowry at East Central University, Ada, Oklahoma. Thanks are also due Linda and D. J. Gerbrandt, J. B. Toews, and Walter Gomez for providing information and insights. Ruby Kroeker Bayless graciously helped me translate some of the Kohfeld material. The patience and forebearance of my wife Lily during the three years I worked on this project will forever be appreciated.

Marvin E. Kroeker
Ada, OK

Prologue

One day in the mid-1890s, a stocky young Mennonite stepped off the Rock Island train onto the dusty streets of Marlow, Indian Territory. As the train resumed its journey south toward the Texas line, Abraham Jacob Becker set his sights westward toward the Wichita Mountains. He caught a ride on a stagecoach that set out across the unbroken and treeless plains of the Kiowa-Comanche-Apache reservation. As far as his eyes could see, the land around him was a sea of grass, dotted occasionally with herds of grazing cattle. The route Becker followed led him to Fort Sill, where he made inquiries about the location of a recently established mission station among the Comanche Indians. The instructions he received led him off the post for about seven miles, but he found nothing. Traveling on foot, he continued his search by following a trail westward for approximately fifteen miles. He was finally forced to bed down for the night on Blue Beaver Creek.

The next morning Becker stopped at the home of an Indian and asked, "Where find Jesus man?" The Indian did not understand English. Fortunately, a Mexican nearby could answer his question. He told Becker that a "little man with little whiskers" lived some seven miles to the northwest. With new spring in his legs, Becker headed in the direction that he hoped would lead to his destination. But his troubles were not over. A snorting herd of some two hundred Texas longhorns suddenly emerged from a timbered area and charged. Frantically the young man waved his bundle, hoping to scare them off. He sought in vain for a tree to climb. The thundering herd stopped momentarily, but then charged again, almost completely surrounding him. When the ill-humored, long-horned steers began to paw the ground and swarm menacingly around him, the aspiring Mennonite preacher fell to his knees in fervent prayer. Suddenly Becker heard a loud commotion. When he raised his head he saw the herd stampeding at full speed away from him toward Blue Beaver Creek. What was already an eventful trip had been turned into an unforgettable experience.

Becker continued his journey westwardly, keeping his eyes on the beautiful mountain range to his right. It was unusual to find such imposing granite outcroppings on the open plains. He had never seen anything like this in Minnesota or Kansas where his family had lived before coming to Oklahoma. True, there were the Glass, or Gloss, Mountains near where he had staked his claim to a quarter section of land in the Cherokee Outlet "Land Run" of 1893, but they were not as impressive as these rugged elevations. His parents had told him about the spectacular Caucasus Mountains near Wohldemfuerst in the Kuban region of Russia where he was born on February 25, 1872. But his family moved to America in 1875, so he had no personal recollections of life or terrain in the land of the czars.

A two-hour walk finally brought Abraham J. Becker to his destination: the makeshift tent home of Mennonite Brethren missionaries Henry and Elizabeth Kohfeld. He had come to spend several months with them, to help build a frame residence and chapel on the grounds of the newly established Post Oak Mission to the Comanche Indians. Little did he realize that five years later he and his wife Magdalena would come to Post Oak Mission to begin lifelong missionary careers among the Native Americans of southwestern Oklahoma.[1]

The Search for a Mission

The Mennonite Brethren branch of the Anabaptist/Mennonite religious movement originated in 1860 in the Molotschna Colony of South Russia. One of its prominent founders and first ministers was Jacob P. Becker (sometimes spelled Bekker), the father of Abraham J. Becker. Beginning in 1874, the loss of military exemptions and special privileges protecting their Germanic cultural life caused a large number of Mennonites to emigrate to the United States and Canada.

In 1879 a Conference of the Mennonite Brethren Church of North America was organized. Ten years later, mission-minded leaders resolved to begin "foreign" missionary activities among the Indians. China and India, it was believed, were beyond the financial means of the fledgling denomination. The first steps were to find a missionary candidate, and then a mission field where he could work. This proved to be difficult and time-consuming. A young seminarian, John Berg, agreed to serve but was later forced to withdraw because of illness. A visit by two church leaders to tribes in Arizona and New Mexico proved fruitless. But at the church's an-

Abraham J. Becker as a child with his grandmother in Russia. Abraham was three years old when the Becker family emigrated to the United States. Credit: Archives & Manuscripts Division of the Oklahoma Historical Society.

nual conference in 1894, held in Hamilton, Nebraska, it was reported that Henry Kohfeld, a Kansas school teacher, had agreed to serve as missionary if a field could be located. The conference directed Kohfeld to search for a location in Oklahoma Territory, and designated limited funds for that purpose. [1]

Henry Kohfeld was born in Rudnerwiede, South Russia; he came to America in 1877 at age fourteen. His parents settled on a farm south of Lehigh, Kansas. As a young man he was baptized and joined the Mennonite Brethren Church at Goessel, Kansas. Kohfeld attended schools at Halstead and Florence, Kansas, hoping to become a teacher or preacher. While at Halstead he befriended an Arapaho Indian from Oklahoma named Henry Miles, a student in a Mennonite boarding school.[2] The General Conference Mennonite Church, a body separate from the Mennonite Brethren, had established mission stations among the Cheyenne and Arapaho Indians of Indian Territory in 1880 and, as part of their program to prepare teachers and workers for reservation mission schools, sent some Indian youth to Kansas to be educated while working on Mennonite farms.[3] Henry Miles was one of these students.

On the farm Miles harrowed, helped with the threshing, and prayed to Jesus "every night make us walk good way." In school he studied in the Third Reader, read gospel stories, and learned arithmetic, geography, and writing. On Sundays Miles and his friends attended Mennonite Sunday school and church services because "we like to walk on the good road."[4] Henry Kohfeld was impressed with the young man's sincere desire to prepare himself for service among his own people and nurtured him in the Christian faith. Tragically, Miles died before he could fulfill his goal. Kohfeld never forgot his first contact with a Native American. After completing a teacher training program, he taught school for six years, the last two in the Gnadenau district south of Hillsboro, Kansas. On August 21, 1892 he married Elizabeth Unruh, born on March 23, 1870 to Mennonite parents in Michalin, Poland.[5]

The appointment of Kohfeld launched an aggressive search for a mission site in Oklahoma. Consultations with General Conference Mennonite Church missionaries in Oklahoma—Rudolph Petter at Cantonment and John J. Kliewer at Shelly—apparently encouraged the Mennonite Brethren to seek a field in the southwestern part of the territory. Although the date is uncertain, it appears that in summer of 1895 a delegation consisting of Rev. Abraham Schellenberg and Rev. John F. Harms left Hillsboro, Kansas for Shelly, located on the Washita River near the present town of Corn. They were met here by Kohfeld who had preceded them. Missionary Kliewer said that the American Baptists were holding a camp meeting at Elk Creek, a Kiowa mission site located forty miles south, and suggested they go there for guidance.

Joined by Abraham Richert, elder in the Washita (later Corn) Mennonite Brethren Church, the delegation traveled to Elk Creek, where they were cordially received by J. S. Murrow, the supervisor of American Baptist missions, and Elton Cyrus Deyo, missionary to the Comanche Indians. They informed the Mennonites that the main area still untouched by Christian missionary work was the western section of the Kiowa-Comanche Reservation. The Baptists had tried to establish a station there but were unable to get permission of the leading Comanche chief, Quanah Parker. Murrow and Deyo encouraged the Mennonites to take up the challenge. After reading scripture and praying for guidance, the group returned to Shelly and made arrangements to send Kohfeld to Fort Sill to open negotiations with officials at a subagency of the Indian Bureau there.[6]

The following morning Rev. Isaak Harms and Peter Bergman, leaders in the Washita church, transported Kohfeld by wagon to the agency office at Fort Sill. There they learned that a quarter section of land for a mission site would likely be granted if the Mennonites obtained the signed approval of Chief Parker and other tribal leaders. While the missionary conferred with the agent, Harms and Bergman proceeded to a nearby grove of trees where they planned to camp for the night. When Kohfeld went to join them later, he could not find them anywhere. Panic gripped him when he saw at least a hundred oxen milling about under the trees where he expected to find his friends. Enveloped by night in a threatening and unfamiliar place in Indian country, he fled to Fort Sill where he found lodging. "Facing dangers and fear in the middle of the night was my introduction to life in the land of the heathen," he later wrote. After a good night's rest, Kohfeld located the other two men camped about a quarter of a mile from the grove where the oxen had frightened him. His friends had spent a restless night speculating about his failure to arrive. Relieved that he was safe, the two now headed for home, sixty miles north, leaving Kohfeld behind to pursue his mission.[7]

The missionary's immediate goal was to gain the approval of tribal leaders for a mission site. It had been made clear that without Quanah Parker's mark on an agreement, no mission would be established. A long history of Comanche-white hostility complicated Kohfeld's task.

The Comanches, whose goodwill Kohfeld now sought, had arrived on the reservation some two decades earlier. Members of the Shoshonean branch of the Uto-Aztecan language family, they once resided west of the Rockies in the Great Plateau region. Sometime during the seventeenth century they moved from their northern home-

Southwestern Oklahoma

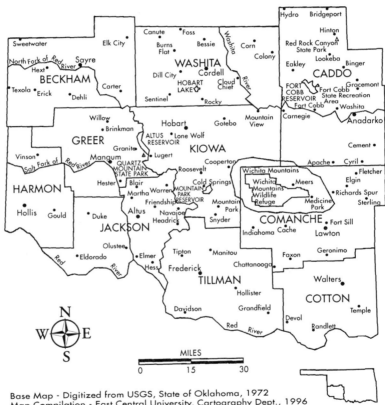

Base Map - Digitized from USGS, State of Oklahoma, 1972
Map Compilation - East Central University, Cartography Dept., 1996

lands and gradually spread south and east; by the end of the century they had reached the southwestern edge of the Southern Plains. Here they made their first contact with whites—the Spaniards settled on the upper Rio Grande. Around 1700 the Comanches acquired horses. Soon they were renowned as the continent's greatest horsemen. The horses gave them new mobility and laid the foundation for the buf-falo-hunting culture that overspread the Great Plains. It made them more efficient hunters and raiders. Comanche warriors became some of the most feared fighters in the American West.

The name Comanche is the hispanicized version of the Ute word Komantcia, meaning "Anyone Who Fights Me All The Time." The name they gave themselves, however, was Nermernuh, "The People." The Comanches' basic political unit was the band. Unlike many Plains Indians, the Comanches had no clan structure or rigid band lines; thus individuals could readily move from one band to another. As many as thirteen different bands existed during historic times. Each operated in an autonomous fashion, never joining together as a unified tribe for purposes of tribal hunts, religious ceremonies, or socializing.

The Comanches have been identified as among the least reli-gious of all the western Indians. They had no dogma, no priestly class, no organized religious system. Until the adoption of the peyote religion sometime in the last half of the nineteenth century, there were no common religious ceremonies, not even the Sun Dance, practiced by most of the Plains tribes. Their religion was largely individualistic, leading to great diversity in faith and expression of beliefs. Comanche afterlife was somewhere beyond the setting sun where there was no want, suffering, or sorrow. In this sacred paradise, they would con-tinue to follow the chase but warfare would be absent.

Comanches believed in a Great Spirit who led the forces of good, and they worshipped the sun, earth, and moon. An Evil Spirit, ac-cording to some Comanches, controlled the forces of evil, but was not as strong as the Great Spirit. There was also a belief in other living spirits, or supernaturals. The Comanches' religion taught them to be courageous, loyal, generous to friends, and to lead an upright life. This would result in a happy eternal existence after death.[8]

Like the other tribes of the Great Plains, the Comanches reached their peak of power, wealth, and influence in the early 1800s. They made a lasting alliance with the Kiowas and then came to hold sway over a large territory east of the Rockies and south of the Arkansas River. Hostile Indian tribes, Spaniards, Mexicans, and Americans entered this area, which the Spaniards called "Comanchéria", at their peril. Comanche hunting and raiding parties ranged far into New Mexico, Texas, and Northern Mexico, terrorizing frontier settlements. Raids were generally of three types: those inspired by attacks of the whites and seeking revenge, those looking for horses and other loot, and those seeking to drive encroaching whites away from their domain. Frontier settlers were no match for the swiftly moving raiders who struck isolated settlements, killed inhabitants, stole property, and frequently abducted women and children. Young captives were sometimes adopted into a band and raised by Comanche families who had lost children in raids by settlers or soldiers.

A raid May 9, 1836 at Fort Parker, Texas had significant ramifications for later Mennonite missionary efforts in Oklahoma. A party of Comanches gained entrance to the stockade, killed five men, wounded several women, and carried off two women and three small children. Among those seized was nine-year-old Cynthia Ann Parker, the future mother of chief Quanah Parker.

When the United States acquired Texas in 1845 and the Mexican Cession in 1848, it inherited a growing problem in Comanche-white relations. Neither Spain, Mexico nor the Texas Republic had been able to control the Comanches and their Kiowa allies. The United States likewise found these elusive and fearsome Indians difficult to subjugate. The struggle of the United States Army against the Comanches would rage intermittently for two decades before massive military force and the destruction of the buffalo would finally end their nomadic way of life.[9]

By 1850 Congress had established the general policy principles and the bureaucracy whereby Indian affairs were administered. Policies were formulated through a series of statutes and a treaty system inherited from colonial times. Originally, Indians were assigned as a responsibility of the Secretary of War, and in 1824 an Office of Indian Affairs was established within the War Department. In the 1830s a commissioner of Indian affairs was authorized, along with a field force of agents and subagents, interpreters, and other employees. In 1849 Indian affairs were transferred from the War Department to the Department of the Interior, where they remain to this day.

The basic objective of early federal Indian policies was to assure the orderly advance of the frontier. If it came down to a question of orderliness versus advancement, however, events soon demonstrated that the latter would clearly win . If Native Americans were willing to assimilate, the federal government was prepared to support such efforts. Congress also promised, in a 1789 law, to protect Indian rights to land. The statute stated that "the utmost good faith shall always be observed towards the Indians; their land and property shall never be taken from them without their consent." However, the government's stated policy to assimilate Indians and protect their rights often conflicted with the frontiersmen's policy. To white frontier farmers, hungry for land, Indians were useless and dangerous people who should make way for them . Wherever they refused, war resulted, and invariably federal troops were dispatched to help break resistance, even in those areas where the government had not cleared Indian rights to land.

Policy concerning the Indian peoples was, therefore, ambiguous and contradictory. On the one hand, there was the "official" policy which seemed fair and just, and on the other, the dynamic of force and conquest, usually followed because of pressure from the white majority. The Indian Removal Policy, implemented by President Andrew Jackson in 1830, is an example of the federal gvernment adopting the frontiersmen's policy as its own. All eastern Indians, including the Five Civilized Tribes, were forced to move to the region west of the Mississippi. This ended Indian resistance east of the river. But it did not end the Indian wars. The new Indian Country was soon invaded by settlers moving westward where the Comanches and other tribes were determined to hold their lands.[10]

Federal relations with the Comanches began in 1835 with the signing of a treaty at Camp Holmes in Indian Territory. The bands agreed to allow safe passage of American citizens across their lands and pledged to maintain peace with the recently arrived Five Civilized Tribes. This treaty did not deter the Comanche bands in their habitual raiding activities in Texas, whose residents they considered their mortal enemies. In 1853 the Comanches, Kiowas, and Kiowa-Apaches signed the Treaty of Fort Atkinson, Kansas, in which they pledged to stop their raiding in Mexico and the United States and to allow the construction of roads and forts in their country. Again, this treaty accomplished little; Comanche war parties continued to raid Texas settlements. Government efforts to solve the problem by segregating peaceful Comanches on Texas reservations and conducting military campaigns against the hostile ones also proved futile. Vengeful Texans made no distinction between peaceful and warlike Indians and called for the extermination of both. During the Civil War, when federal troops were withdrawn from the frontier posts, Comanche and Kiowa war parties forced many Texans to abandon their homes and flee eastward for safety.[11]

Following the Civil War the government tried once again to make peace with the redoubtable Comanches. In the Treaty of Little Arkansas in 1865, government commissioners persuaded some chiefs to give up claims to central Texas, western Kansas, and eastern New Mexico, receiving in exchange annuities and hunting rights to most of the Panhandle of Texas, and that part of Indian Territory west of the ninety-eighth meridian.[12] The official shrinking of the boundaries of Comancheria had begun. As the influx of settlers onto the Great Plains increased, the government inaugurated a policy of moving Indians onto clearly defined and out-of-the-way reservations. Government officials and humanitarians alike agreed that only by forcing Indians to give up their nomadic way of life and to adopt farming and Christianity could they be pacified and truly civilized.

The important Treaty of Medicine Lodge, signed October 21, 1867, established the reservation system for the Comanches and other Southern Plains tribes. By terms of that treaty, the Comanches, Kiowas, and Kiowa-Apaches agreed to relinquish their ranges in the panhandles of Texas and Indian Territory and accept a reservation in southwestern Indian Territory between the Red and Washita rivers. Representatives of the three tribes agreed to give up their nomadic ways, and in general seek to "walk the white man's road." The government in turn promised to provide agents, schools, churches, farms, clothing, and food, until the Indians would be adjusted to a sedentary life. The tribes pledged to refrain from forays against travelers or settlements, and to "never kill or scalp white men, nor attempt to do them any harm."[13]

It took years, and further military force, before all the tribespeople moved to the reservation. The disruptions and turmoil of their last years of freedom took a heavy physical and psychological toll on the Comanches. Their population was down to about 1,500, an estimated 50 percent decline since 1867. The last band to surrender arrived at Fort Sill in 1875 and included Quanah Parker.

Quanah was the son of Peta Nocona, a war chief, and the Cynthia Ann Parker who had been captured as a young girl and adopted by the Comanches. As a young man Quanah followed the buffalo herds, raided Texas settlements, and warred against Indian, Mexican, and white foes. He experienced the loss of both parents before age twelve: his mother was recaptured, against her will , in 1860, and his father, according to Quanah, died two or three years later. He recalled those years as very unhappy ones and developed, understandably, a deep distrust of whites.

Defeated and demoralized, the Comanches were now subjected to a forced acculturation program designed to re-create Indians in the image of whites. Quaker agents, appointed to implement the government's new "peace policy," sought to transform buffalo hunters into farmers. Efforts were made to suppress Indian customs and languages, and to alter their styles of hair and dress to resemble the whites. Indian children were placed in boarding schools, often run like military prisons, where they were made to work and learn the white ways. What the policy makers perceived as enlightened civilization programs, the Indians saw as an ordeal at best and genocide at worst. The agricultural program, both under the Quakers and their successors, met with little success. Inadequate rainfall was the main problem, although a lack of farming skills and desire on the part of the Indians also contributed to the slow progress.[14]

Quanah was a flexible and perceptive young man. He adjusted quickly to the Comanches' new situation, was appointed a chief by the agent, and soon emerged as an influential tribal leader whose views had to be reckoned with on all important reservation matters. He eventually supported the government's educational and agricultural programs and encouraged his people to adapt to their new economic and political realities. Yet he wore his hair long , had multiple wives, and practiced the peyote religion—each in violation of law or government policy. Since Christian churches also vigorously opposed such "heathenish" ways, Quanah, and many Indian traditionalists were not eager to allow white missionaries on the reservation. Henry Kohfeld would have to find a way to overcome those concerns, as well as the resentment over white aggressions of the past, if he was to win Comanche approval for a Mennonite mission among them .[15]

"Here Build Jesus House"

Missionary Henry Kohfeld's initial efforts to gain Comanche support for a mission proved discouraging. From his base at the Deyo Comanche Mission, fifteen miles southwest of Fort Sill, he traveled extensively on horseback across the western section of the reservation seeking to win over the people. Apparently the Indians did not find the black-bearded foreigner, who spoke English with a German accent, very convincing. They made it clear that "even though a Jesus Man and a Jesus House might be all right, neither should be found too close to them or upon their land." After two-and-a-half months of fruitless endeavors, and with his expense account of $150 diminished, the missionary-designate was so frustrated he contemplated giving up. In that "dark hour of temptation," he later related, he fell on his knees on the hot, dry prairie and prayed for guidance. A voice told him not to "flee like a Jonah," but to "put your trust in God who will give you victory."

Reinvigorated, Kohfeld decided to take his plea directly to Chief Quanah Parker, who apparently had been away from home much of this time. The Fort Sill Indian agent, who had given Kohfeld little assistance previously, cooperated by providing an interpreter and a team and wagon. As they made their way toward Quanah's home, Kohfeld promised the interpreter his prized watch for help in persuading the chief to grant land for a mission. Quanah Parker's residence, later called the Star House because of large stars painted on the roof, was located three miles north and two west of present Cache, Oklahoma. This large home had been built with the aid of Texas cattlemen who appreciated his help in arranging pasture leases. Quanah was not at home when Kohfeld and the interpreter arrived, so they explained the purpose of their visit to family members and friends who were present. The interpreter, a Christian convert of the Dutch Reformed Mission, near present Lawton, was probably Howard Whitewolf (White Wolf), identified as a Comanche church leader and an early-day interpreter at the mission. Also involved in tribal politics he would have been acquainted with Quanah.

The interpreter must have been persuasive, for according to Kohfeld's account, when the chief arrived, one of his wives spoke to him about the matter. "My dear husband," she said, "we have lived together twenty years and have been happy. Here is Jesus man, sent from God to build a Jesus House and teach us the way to heaven. If you hinder him, I shall never be happy again." A woman named Tessika, whose husband had considerable influence with Quanah, also interceded on behalf of the missionary's quest.

Chief Parker discussed the issue with some ten to twelve of his tribesmen and reached a decision. He ordered Kohfeld to mount a horse behind an Indian. The chief led the party in a southwesterly direction, racing full speed for several miles over rough terrain and through a creek—a frightening experience Kohfeld would never forget. The horsemen stopped at a prominent post oak tree. Quanah cut several branches off the tree and notched the trunk. He hung the branches on the tree and said, "Here build Jesus House." Kohfeld produced a document authorizing 160 acres of land to be granted the Mennonite Brethren Church for mission purposes and secured the signatures or marks of Quanah and several other headmen of the Comanches. Post Oak Mission was born.

The Mennonite missionary was overwhelmed by the events of the day. "All this occurred the day after my severe, dark hour of testing," he reported. God had done it, Kohfeld was convinced. Nevertheless, he gave his watch to the interpreter.[1]

There is confusion about which of Quanah's wives interceded on behalf of the Mennonite Brethren mission. Her name is not mentioned in Kohfeld's written accounts. Abraham E. Janzen believed it was To-pay (Something Fell) and gave her the credit in a Board of Foreign Missions publication in 1946.[2] This assertion has been repeated in many published accounts. It is highly improbable that the quote, "We have lived together twenty years," came from To-pay. Quanah had taken her as his wife in 1894, after handing over two horses, a carriage and harness, and $50 to another Comanche who also claimed her.[3] Clearly the two had not yet lived happily together for two decades. At the time, the chief had three wives who had been with him for twenty years or more: Weck-e-ah, Cho-ny, and Machet-to-Wooky. Three or four others had been acquired later. Only To-pay seems to have actively participated in activities at Post Oak Mission; she eventually became a baptized member of the church. If this young bride was the intercessor—and there is oral tradition to support that claim—it must be assumed that either Kohfeld's memory, or his interpreter's translation, fell short in providing an accurate account of this event.

Not only did Kohfeld gain permission to establish a mission, he was invited to spend the night at Quanah's house. He was provided a "wonderful supper and sleeping quarters," and through his interpreter preached his first sermon to a Native American audience. He may have pressed his luck since Quanah would remain cool to the missionaries for many years.[4]

The following day Kohfeld presented the document with the Indian signatures to the subagency office at Fort Sill. Official authorization granting the site to the Mennonite Brethren had to come from the commissioner of Indian affairs in Washington, but the prospects for his approval appeared good. The Indian agent at Anadarko, Major Frank Baldwin, told Kohfeld he would personally visit Quanah in three or four weeks to discuss the matter. Kohfeld was invited to go along. On October 21, 1895, Kohfeld wrote Baldwin, reminding him of their conversation some three weeks earlier, and stating that he had presented "the prospect you gave me about the selection I made for our mission" to his board. He wished to know when their meeting with the chief would take place. Baldwin responded that it was impossible for him to set a date since he would be in Washington until the middle of November. Nevertheless, Kohfeld apparently assumed that approval for a mission site was assured and informed his board accordingly.[5]

Kohfeld's information was announced at the annual meeting of the General Conference of the Mennonite Brethren Church, October 28-29, 1895 which, in an interesting coincidence, was convened at Parker, South Dakota. The thirty delegates voted enthusiastically to appropriate $800 for a chapel and residence and $500 a year for missionary Kohfeld's salary. The conference also elected a Foreign Mission Committee, consisting of Abraham Schellenberg, Cornelius P. Wedel, and John F. Harms. As far as the delegates were concerned, Post Oak Mission, the first "foreign" mission field of the denomination's North American branch, was now officially established.[6] However, official government authorization for a mission had not yet come from Washington.

According to Foreign Mission Board accounts, the first two buildings at Post Oak Mission were completed in the fall of 1895. This is inaccurate.[7] It was not until February 26, 1896 that agent Frank Baldwin sent the Mennonites application papers "relative to the establishing of a mission by you on this reservation." He instructed them "to address the Commisssioner of Indian Affairs, through my office, giving him a statement of what you desire in the way of land etc. returning the enclosed papers with such letter."[8]

The Mennonite response was prompt and on March 10 their application was forwarded to the commissioner's office in Washington. In his transmittal letter, Baldwin informed the commissioner that consent of the Comanche headmen had been secured and recommended that the Mennonites be allowed to occupy the quarter section of land requested.[9] John F. Harms, secretary of the mission committee, sent a separate letter to Representative Charles Curtis of Kansas, requesting his support: "If you can give this matter your personal attention and assist us in our effort to obtain permission and the grant, also to urge action upon the matter without any unnecessary delay it will be a great favor and be duly appreciated."[10]

Curtis, chair of the House Committee on Expenditures in the Interior Department, transmitted Harms' letter to D. M. Browning, commissioner of Indian affairs: "I hope you will give this application careful consideration and grant the request if possible. I am acquainted with Mr. Harmes [sic] and know him to be perfectly reliable."[11] The commissioner approved the request, but added a stipulation that threatened to further delay the start of the mission enterprise. The grant of 160 acres of land and authority to erect a chapel and house for a missionary was made contingent on evidence that, in addition to the Comanche leaders, "the consent of the head-men and chiefs representing the other Indians occupying this reservation" had been secured. When such further consent had been obtained, Browning wrote, the agent could "formally set this said tract of 160 acres aside to the Mennonite Brethren Church."[12]

Kohfeld, waiting in Fort Sill for authorization to occupy the proposed mission site, was notified of Browning's stipulation by sub-agent E. F. Burton. Greatly frustrated, the missionary informed Harms that getting the approval of the Kiowa and Apache chiefs could take him many months. Harms immediately dispatched another letter to Representative Curtis, complaining about the notification "to see all the Chiefs of the Kiowas, Commanches and Apaches" in order to get their permission for a mission. He was disappointed by the demand, claiming it would require "several months traveling and much annoyance." He speculated whether the commissioner was deliberately placing "obstacles in the way of mission work among the Indians" and asked his "dear friend" to see what he could do to help. "As the Indians in the neighborhood are all in favor of establishing the mission and as even their chief Quannah Parker has signed our petition, we think that it would be sufficient," he declared.[13] In a cover letter forwarding Harms' correspondence to commissioner Browning, Curtis addressed the directive given to Kohfeld "to see all the Chiefs." He wrote: "I hope unless it is absolutely necessary that this requirement will not be made of him."[14]

Political influence brought speedy results, as seen in a second letter by Browning to Baldwin, dated April 14, 1896. The commissioner now wrote that it had not been his intention to keep the Mennonites from occupying the land set aside for them. "They can be allowed," he stated, "to take possession of this tract of land and commence work as soon as they desire." Furthermore, he also directed the agent to obtain the consent of the Kiowa and other Indian leaders "at such time as will suit your convenience." This would "relieve the missionary of any further trouble in the matter." [15]

The fact that Browning was willing to grant authorization before getting the approval of the Kiowa leaders, an unusual procedure, is an indication of the powerful influence of Representative Curtis, a mixed-blood Kaw Indian who would later serve as vice president of the United States. It also reveals the political stature of Quanah Parker. As long as the Mennonites had the permission of that Comanche chief, the government was not overly concerned about the views of other tribal leaders on the reservation.

On April 20, 1896 agent Baldwin sent the following notice to the Mennonite Brethren Mission Committee: "Under instructions of the Hon. Commissioner of Indian Affairs I am directed to inform you that you can proceed with the erection of buildings etc. necessary for the proper maintenance and continuance of the mission to be located in the Comanche country. . . ." The grant of a quarter section of land had been approved and would be recorded in the land book of the Kiowa and Comanche Reservation. [16]

Baldwin was miffed by the content of Harms' letter to Curtis. He wrote Browning that Kohfeld's statements to Harms "were very much in error." In the first place, the missionary had been informed that it would be necessary to get the approval of the Kiowas as well as the Comanches. Furthermore, once he had obtained the signatures of the Comanches, it would have been a simple matter for him to get the signatures of the main Kiowa leaders. He complained that when church groups were given any privilege on the reservation "they except [sic] the agent to relieve them of all labor or responsibility in the matter." [17]

Despite this sour note, the Mennonites were now free to build a Comanche "Jesus House" on the Post Oak Mission grounds.

Laying the Foundation:
The Early Kohfeld Years

Henry and Elizabeth Kohfeld, along with a young daughter, moved to the Oklahoma mission field sometime in the spring of 1896. They first traveled to Marlow, where they spent a week making arrangements for needed construction. This bustling frontier town was located on the old Chisholm Trail just east of the Kiowa-Comanche Reservation. It had sprung up four years earlier when the Rock Island Railroad laid track through the area. Situated fifty miles from the Post Oak Mission site, it would serve as the trade center for missionaries until the reservation was opened to white settlement. A twenty-three-mile unimproved trail connected Marlow with Fort Sill, an important army post established in 1869 to police the reservation Indians.

Elizabeth Kohfeld, wife of Henry Kohfeld.   *Henry Kohfeld, missionary to the Comanche*
                                                        Indians of southwestern Oklahoma
They were the first missionary couple sponsored by the Conference of the Mennonite Brethren Church of North America.
Credit: The Center for Mennonite Brethren Studies, Fresno, CA

Kohfeld obtained lumber for a chapel and living quarters from sawmills in the Rush Springs vicinity. He paid $10 per thousand square feet for number 2 lumber and $15 per thousand for finish lumber. He hired freighters to deliver construction supplies to the building site, twenty-five miles west of Fort Sill. Volunteer construction workers were recruited from Korn (anglicized to Corn after 1918 due to World War I inspired anti-German bias), a rapidly growing Mennonite community established in Washita County in 1893.[1] The building project marked the beginning of a close relationship between members of the Korn Mennonite Brethren Church and the Comanche Post Oak Mission. Others, such as Mennonite Brethren Church member Abraham Becker from Fairview, also donated their carpentry skills. [2] With these preliminary arrangements in place, the Kohfelds moved to the Post Oak site, erected a tent as their temporary home, and began to "get the taste of what it meant to live like Indians."[3] At the meeting of the Mennonite Brethren General Conference in fall 1896, a report from Kohfeld was read, indicating the construction of mission buildings was almost completed. [4]

It had been difficult to locate and get approval for a mission; it now proved even more difficult to convince the Comanches of their need for the Christian religion. It would be twelve years before the Mennonites baptized their first convert. The fact that the Indians consented to give them 160 acres of rocky land none of the tribespeople had chosen to occupy was no indication of their openness to the gospel. It was the Baptists, not the Indians, who had invited the Mennonite Brethren to come preach Christianity to the "heathen" Comanches. Most of the tribespeople seemed content with their traditional beliefs and practices. A long history of encroachment on their hunting lands, warfare, race prejudice, reservation confinement, and the shattering of their entire culture, inclined them against the acceptance of white Christian civilization. According to one Indian: "White man heap cheat and no good; maybe Jesus Man no good." [5]

The Indians' attitude toward Kohfeld was marked by indifference, suspicion, annoyance, and mild hostility. Quanah, whose home was only a few miles northeast of Post Oak, initially was not openly hostile, but he was not supportive either. Kohfeld was convinced that the chief discouraged his people from attending church services at the mission. Along with other Christian missionaries, the Mennonites taught that there was only one road to salvation and eternal life, and that was the "Jesus Road," as taught in the Bible. Many Comanches, including Quanah, participated in peyote ceremonies as part of their religious expression. Peyote is a turnip-shaped fruit of a cactus which grows in northern Mexico and parts of the southwestern United States. The peyote fruit, called the button, contains a halucinogenic element which reportedly produces visions and dreams. In some places peyote is locally called mescal, a term also applied to the beans from a leguminous shrub. Although practices varied, a peyote cult worship service often included, besides ingesting peyote, individual and group singing, praying, drumming, meditating, and performing mystical rites. Peyote adherents told the missionaries that Ta-a'pah (God) had given the Bible to whites to speak to them but that he communicated with Indians through peyote. The hostility of missionaries to some of the natives' traditional beliefs and customs hindered their effectiveness. Although the local Indian agents generally agreed that Quanah's use of peyote was not a drug problem, church groups consistently pressured the government to abolish its use. The resentment produced over this issue had to be overcome before Rev. Kohfeld could expect to make any inroads into Quanah's band.

Missionary Kohfeld learned quickly that the Indians could not readily be enticed to come to traditional Sunday church services. Usually the only attenders were a few local white cowboys. Of the handful of Indians who might attend, most could not understand English. Throughout his tenure, Kohfeld found it difficult to acquire interpreters, even for pay. Eventually he was able to conduct simple conversations with the people in their native language but he was not able to preach effectively in Comanche. He spent only one month in concentrated language study. With the aid of an interpreter, the Lord's Prayer, the Ten Commandments, and several Bible stories and parables were translated into Comanche writing.[6]

Since few Indians would come to the mission to hear him preach, Kohfeld decided to take his message to them at their homes or campgrounds. When the Indians gathered to receive their payments from the government they frequently spent time visiting and playing cards. Often, they gambled on the card games. The Kohfelds entered their tents to sing, pray, and proclaim their need of salvation. This approach was bold, dramatic, and, for most of the Indians, offensive. Kohfeld lamented, "Only those who by God's grace were driven into a corner were willing to listen to us." The rest continued their gambling or stalked off the premises.[7]

A terminally ill Indian became what Kohfeld called the "first sheaf" harvested at Post Oak Mission. Hughes was a young man afflicted with tuberculosis who became attached to the missionaries. They allowed him to move in with them to receive physical and spiritual care. Shortly before his death he accepted the "Jesus Way" and, reflecting the Kohfelds' influence, requested a Christian burial. Hughes' family concurred and so a grave site was chosen on a plot of ground near the chapel. This was the beginning of what became the Post

Oak Mission Cemetery. It is believed that this first grave was dug in the summer of 1898.

In traditional Comanche burial customs, as explained to Herwanna Becker Bernard by a Comanche informant, the body was wrapped in a blanket and laid on the back of a horse behind a rider. The rider then traveled up a mountain searching for a cave, recess, or crevice in which to place the body. Once placed in its tomb, the body was covered completely with stones. The "pallbearer" then solemnly returned to the camp. Meanwhile, the mourners buried all of the deceased's personal possessions "to erase the last sad memories." On a hillside outside the camp the chief mourner slashed his arms "in a ritual meant to intensify grief and to symbolize a mutual suffering with the dead." When Kohfeld first arrived on the reservation, the Quahada Comanches still followed this tradition, burying their dead in the Wichita Mountains.

Through the teachings and influence of Rev. Kohfeld, and later the Beckers, the Indians began to accept the Christian mode of burying the dead. The missionaries at Post Oak were soon called upon to conduct many funeral services. In the early years they also made the coffins and dug the graves. These occasions were their best opportunities to explain to a more receptive audience the Christian view of salvation, death, resurrection, and the promise of eternal life.[8]

A second deathbed convert was an elderly woman related to one of Quanah's wives. The woman told Kohfeld that she had a dream in which she had died and was facing Ta-a'pah (God) on the day of judgment. She awakened screaming because she knew she was very sinful. Kohfeld persuaded her to accept the "Jesus Way." After that she declined the services of the medicine man, declaring she was ready to die and go to heaven. This woman was the second person buried at Post Oak. Since neither of these first converts were well enough to be baptized by immersion, they could not become the first members of a mission church.[9]

Before Henry Kohfeld came to Oklahoma he suffered from indigestion, especially if he ate meat or fatty foods. Soon after his arrival he encountered a camp of Kiowa men who invited him to join them in a meal. He agreed, although he said later that the stench of meat hanging in the hot sun, and the sight of fry bread and dirty coffee, almost turned his stomach. The men asked Kohfeld if he wanted to say grace over the food. Although feeling far from comfortable, he thanked God for the hospitality of his hosts and for the food they had prepared. He realized he dare not refuse to eat what he had just asked

God to bless. To his surprise, Kohfeld suffered no adverse aftereffects. In fact, his stomach problems totally disappeared and he became an avid eater of beef. He described this as one of several miracles he experienced during his early days as a missionary.[10]

Two children were born to the Kohfelds during their time on the reservation. Their first child, Emma, was born in Kansas; she was joined by a sister, Bertha, and a brother, Henry. Interviewed in 1994, at age ninety-five, Henry Kohfeld Jr. still had vivid and fond memories of his boyhood on the Comanche reservation. He attended school with Comanche children, was their playmate, and learned their language.[11]

Beginning in 1897 single women called deaconesses were sent to assist the missionaries with household duties and other mission-related work. Maria Regier from the Ebenezer Mennonite Brethren Church near Buhler, Kansas was the first deaconess appointed. Two years later Katharina Penner of the Ebenfeld Mennonite Brethren Church near Hillsboro, Kansas joined her. After the arrival of the deaconesses, the practice of serving meals to the Indians at the Sunday mission services was instituted. This increased attendance and also led to more cordial relations. Sewing classes were begun and home visitation increased. "It is a good way to develop trust and understanding when we can visit and work together," Maria Regier reported. When John F. Harms visited the mission in summer 1899 he brought 340 yards of cotton print for the Indians. Regier told the recipients, "Christians have sent this to you out of love for you, and they are praying that you might accept the Jesus Way so that they can meet you someday in heaven." Those few who could understand her seemed impressed.

The Post Oak mission staged a major feast to celebrate Christmas 1899. Mission personnel prepared for 100 to 120 people, although they did not know how many to expect. By ten o'clock that morning Indians began to arrive from all directions, some on horseback, many in wagons. Rev. Kohfeld directed them into the chapel where he preached a sermon condemning the "Sin Way" and extolling the "Jesus Way." He believed that the message, "delivered with great earnestness," was well received because there "was not the slightest disturbance or disorderliness that occurred." At times the Indians did not observe the decorum practiced in white churches; they lounged in the pews, snored, and spoke audibly to each other. During the service Mrs. Kohfeld and Maria Regier frantically prepared more food because 170 Indians had appeared, far more than they had prepared for. "But the Lord blessed the food so that there was enough for all, and some left over," a relieved Maria Regier reported. A public relations disaster for Post Oak had been averted.

Following the meal the crowd returned to the chapel for an explanation of the Christian meaning of Christmas and the distribution of gifts. Funds for the Christmas celebration had been raised by the Oklahoma and Kansas Mennonite Brethren churches. The workers considered the event highly successful, declaring that the food and gifts left a very good impression. Although exhausted by the end of the day, Regier predicted that the experience would lead to conversions. One woman had asked her about this "Jesus Way" she and the missionary spoke of. She tried to explain it but regretted she could not communicate in Comanche. The language barrier appears to have been a major factor in the lack of success in winning converts in the early years at Post Oak.[12]

Deaconess Regier returned to Kansas in 1900 to care for her sick mother. She married Dietrich D. Peters in 1894; she died in childbirth the following year. As the first deaconess of the Mennonite Brethren Church, she left a positive mark on the fledgling mission enterprise in southwestern Oklahoma.

Katharina Penner devoted much of her time to the home visitation program and prepared meals for the Indians on Sundays. She purchased a horse and a two-wheeled cart for transportation to the Indian residences and campsites. During the long, hot summer months she could be seen bouncing across the barren countryside, seeking persons who might be in need of her love and care. Her work was hard and often frustrating and in 1905, when her prayers "for any opportunity of having a happy marriage" were answered, she resigned her position. Penner found the answer to her prayers in Henry Suderman, a member of her home church in Kansas. Together they provided financial support for Post Oak until her death in 1933.[13]

Establishing good rapport with the Comanches was only one of the difficulties facing Kohfeld. For a number of years he also had to cope with an inadequate source of water. Water frequently had to be hauled from a location about four miles away. One day during the dry summer of 1898, the missionary, a firm believer in the power of prayer, secluded himself in a closet to seek divine guidance on this matter. He was liberated when he heard the voice of God say, "Today you shall find water." How and where was not revealed to him.

Just then the interpreter who was helping him with his language study arrived. Kohfeld told him he was concerned about the water problem and had been praying about it. The Indian said he had noticed a green spot of grass in the otherwise dry field north of the chapel. They walked about 200 yards to the location and began to dig. Within fifteen minutes they had found "enough water to supply 100 head of cattle." This spring, eventually aided by a windmill, provided an excellent water supply for the mission. Kohfeld considered this event as another miracle from God.[14]

The illness of Chief Quanah Parker's son Harold led to improved relations between the Mennonites and the Comanche leader. The son of Cho-ny, Harold was a bright young man who attended the Indian school at Carlisle, Pennsylvania. After his return he managed his father's correspondence, reading him the mail, and helping him write responses. A handsome man with a promising future, he was considered the chief's pride and joy. Harold contracted tuberculosis, however, and his condition deteriorated to the point where he was not expected to survive. When Rev. Kohfeld heard the news, he paid him a visit. He discovered about thirty Indians assembled under an arbor in the chief's yard. He was invited to take a seat next to Quanah and answer questions about the Mennonite religion. Harold's illness had caused some of them to wonder if there was help to be found in Christianity. Kohfeld explained the basic tenets of the Christian faith and the believer's hope of eternal life after death. He was quizzed for about an hour, after which Quanah reportedly said, "I see, I see now what I never could understand or grasp before."

Quanah then took Kohfeld to Harold for a visit of about thirty minutes. After hearing some words of comfort and Christian hope, the frail son indicated that he wanted to accept the "Jesus Way." The father, deeply moved, fell to his knees beside the missionary, who offered a prayer for Harold. The chief grasped Kohfeld's hand and thanked him for his prayers and concern.

Three days later Harold Parker was taken to Carrizozo, New Mexico for treatment; Quanah's first wife, an Apache, came from that area and he still had contacts there. Harold died shortly after his arrival. His body was returned to Post Oak Mission for burial. The grief-stricken father stated that his son had talked frequently in his last days about the things missionary Kohfeld had told him. Harold said he was happy he had found God's love. For that reason the chief wanted to bury him at the mission cemetery rather than at Fort Sill.

At the funeral service Rev. Kohfeld told the chief and the large audience in attendance that they should not despair, for Harold was now at peace, "resting on God's bosom." God's own son had died to bring salvation to the Indians, he said and Harold's death could be the way to bring his people to the eternal life he was now enjoying. After the burial Quanah asked the people to go back into the chapel. He stepped behind the pulpit, took the Bible in his hand, and addressed his fellow Comanches. He had been to Washington many times, he stated, and had met presidents and senators, but never had he heard anything as comforting or inspiring as what he heard from the Bible and "this dear missionary today." He urged his people to come to the mission every Sunday and listen to God's word. Here was the way to the heavenly home. Harold had told him he loved Jesus and wanted to go home, and God had granted his wish; he was now there. Then Quanah said a prayer and departed.

After Harold's death, according to Kohfeld, Quanah never again discouraged anyone from participating in mission activities. The Sunday after the funeral the chief arrived at Post Oak with twenty Indians in tow. Although he rarely appeared thereafter, numerous members of the extended Parker family eventually became baptized members of the church.[15]

Missionary Assistant and Field Matron: The Beckers' Ministry Begins

I n 1901, because of increasing activities and greater Indian participation at Post Oak Mission, the Foreign Mission Board of the Mennonite Brethren Church appointed Abraham J. Becker as a missionary assistant to the Kohfelds. After helping with construction of the mission buildings at Post Oak in 1896, Becker had returned home to complete his education. On October 27, 1897 he married Magdalena Hergert at Fairview, Oklahoma. The daughter of a minister, Magdalena was born August 4, 1878 in the Ebenfeld community near Hillsboro, Kansas. In 1894, shortly after the Cherokee Strip was opened, she moved with her parents to Fairview. At age 16 she was baptized and joined the Süd-Hoffnungsfeld (South Hopefield) Mennonite Brethren Church.

Magdalena and A.J. Becker, circa 1897
Credit: The Center for Mennonite Brethren Studies, Fresno CA

Following his marriage, Becker attended McPherson College in Kansas for two years, preparing himself for service in the church. The German department at McPherson College, with Mennonite Brethren teachers, was the first Mennonite Brethren training school for Christian workers. At the 1897 meeting of the Mennonite Brethren

General Conference it was decided to establish a school at Post Oak, believing it would contribute to the progress of the mission work. Becker was asked to be superintendent. This project, however, was dropped after the costs of erecting dormitory facilities were ascertained. Instead of going to Post Oak to open a school, the Beckers took on a missionary ministry that would last for a lifetime.[1]

In December 1901, two months after his appointment as missionary, Becker traveled to Post Oak to confer with Kohfeld and make housing arrangements for his family. He started to construct a house, but when he left it was far from finished. On March 7, 1902 he brought his wife and two sons, Daniel and William, to the station in a covered wagon. Enroute from Fairview, they were forced to spend one night on the open prairie north of Anadarko. "We froze terrible that night," he recalled. Furthermore, one of the horses went lame the next morning, requiring Becker to help the other horse pull the wagon up some of the steeper inclines.[2] Along with a salary of $400 a year, the conference had appropriated funds to build a house for the new missionary. Since Becker was known to have carpentry skills, it was anticipated he would do most of the work. To help him finish his house Becker called on his hired farm hand at Fairview for assistance. Not only did David C. Peters help build the house, he remained at the mission until 1915, serving as a valued worker. He was treated as a member of the family, one of several persons to merit that favor over the years.[3]

The Beckers' arrival coincided with the beginnings of the tumultuous period associated with implementation of the allotment program on the Kiowa-Comanche Reservation. With passage of the General Allotment Act in 1887, the government began a policy of parceling out reservation lands to individual Indians–ownership would be in the hands of individuals, not the tribe. This was a further effort to detribalize the Native Americans and turn them into independent self-sufficient farmers and, eventually, citizens of the United States. To accomodate western land hunger, not all of the reservation land was allotted to the Indian residents; instead, millions of acres of the "surplus" land on Oklahoma reservations were made available to non-Indians.

Chief Parker had reluctantly accepted the provisions of an allotment agreement negotiated with the government in 1892, but through shrewd bargaining and a surprising display of business acumen won better terms than originally dictated. He then fought hard to delay implementation of this land grabbing program as long as possible.[4]

Lone Wolf, a Kiowa leader, filed a lawsuit against the government, seeking to prevent allotment and the opening of reservation lands to whites, but to no avail. Thus, some of the reservation lands were assigned to individual Indians and the "surplus" opened to non-Indian settlers through a lottery procedure.[5] Tent cities and towns sprang up overnight. Lawton was founded August 6, 1901, seven months before the Beckers came to Oklahoma. Cache, located about eight miles southeast of Post Oak Mission, was established in 1902; Indiahoma, five miles southwest of the mission, emerged the same year.

Oklahoma Land Openings

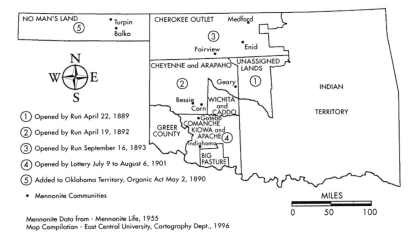

(1) Opened by Run April 22, 1889

(2) Opened by Run April 19, 1892

(3) Opened by Run September 16, 1893

(4) Opened by Lottery July 9 to August 6, 1901

(5) Added to Oklahoma Territory, Organic Act May 2, 1890

• Mennonite Communities

Mennonite Data from - Mennonite Life, 1955
Map Compilation - East Central University, Cartography Dept., 1996

Although many Mennonites participated in the earlier Oklahoma land openings, only a small number of them settled on lands within the old Kiowa-Comanche Reservation boundaries. No Mennonite settlements developed in the Post Oak Mission area. In 1902-03 four small Mennonite church communities were established in the Gotebo vicinity in northern Kiowa County. Only two of these, one a Mennonite Brethren congregation, survived past 1921. The German-Russian Mennonites who came to Oklahoma were poor people in search of better economic opportunities. If the acquisition of lands wrested earlier from poor Indians posed a moral dilemma for the Mennonites, it did not noticeably deter them.

The allotment process led to the relocation of many Indians served by the mission. Kohfeld suggested that the mission itself might have to move to be more readily accessible to the Comanches. The turmoil and disruptions of the new circumstances caused a decline in attendance and interest in mission activities. Rev. Becker was struck, when he arrived at the mission, by the "coldness of the hearts" of the Indians. [6] The Quahada Comanches, among whom the Mennonite missionaries worked, had been the last of that tribe to surrender to reservation life. They were considered to be more resistant to white Christian influences than any other band.

The failure to get any Indians to join the church through baptism proved discouraging. With two missionary couples, a deaconess, and a farm worker on the field, it was necessary to show some results in order to maintain the financial support of the church constituency. A candidate for baptism was finally found: David Peters, Becker's white employee, converted to Christianity after his arrival at the mission. Becker decided to invite the Indians to a daylong celebration, which would include a feast and the baptismal ceremony. Since the Indians had never seen a baptism the missionaries wanted to make it an educational and inspirational experience which they might be encouraged to follow. On Sunday, June 8, 1902, forty-five Indians gathered at Post Oak. Beans, a large black kettle of cooked beef, coffee, and Mennonite zwieback (rolls) were prepared for the occasion. Kohfeld preached a sermon before the meal, and after, explained the meaning of baptism as best he could in the Comanche language. The baptism took place in a pond Peters helped construct on the mission farm. The Indians watched the proceedings with great interest and curiosity. Some had the idea the missionary would pull the husky, six-foot-two-inch white man through the water by a rope. Before proceeding with the immersion, the slightly built Kohfeld quietly asked Peters to help him out as much as possible so they would not both drown. Following the baptism some Indians said, "God's way is a good way," but it would still be five years before any of them were willing to follow that "way" into the baptismal pond.

Peters frequently prayed and gave testimony of his faith in church, so the Indians called him "Little Preacher." [7] They named Kohfeld Tia-cho-nika, "Little Hat," apparently because he frequently wore a derby hat.[8] Becker, who had a short blond beard, was given the Comanche name To sa-mocho, "White Beard."[9] Magdalena Becker became Tah-pah-see, "Our Older Sister."

Another attempt to stimulate conversions came through the use of native Christian speakers. David Peters was present at a gospel camp meeting near the Red Store where Sanco, a Kiowa, was invited to address a gathering of Comanches. The Kiowa told his Comanche friends that he would relate an experience he had never shared before. It was not easy to talk about it, he said. Some time ago, after listening to the missionary at Rainy Mountain Mission near Gotebo, he decided to follow "God's Road", and agreed to be baptized. Because he had been a singer and helped with the peyote services, a medicine chief pressured him not to join the mission church. A big peyote ceremony was scheduled to take place near Sanco's home. If he did not give up the "Jesus Road" and participate in the ceremony, he was told, the medicine man would pray to the Great Spirit to strike him with a fatal illness. Still he refused.

Sanco found no sleep as the nightlong peyote ceremony began. The sound of the drums and the singing reminded him of the old stories of the powers of medicine chiefs. He was so restless that his wife awoke and said, "Sanco, you are not sleeping, are you sick?" He replied with a loud "NO!" Soon, however, he felt ill and wondered if he might actually die. He took courage when he realized if he died he would go to heaven, "for I am on the road to heaven." Reassured, he fell asleep until sunrise.

Just as he awoke, the medicine man stepped out of his tent, facing the sun, and with outstretched hands called on the Great Spirit to destroy Sanco for leaving the peyote road. "As he prayed thus, blood gushed out of his mouth and he sank forward to the ground." Several men ran into Sanco's tent for water, but when they returned with it the medicine man was dead. Sanco said, "I was baptized that Sunday." He concluded his talk with an admonition: "You Comanches are holding back, what are you afraid of?" This dramatic presentation did not result in an immediate spiritual breakthrough, but it made an emotional impact on the listeners. The seed sown that day, Peters intimates, bore fruit later.[10]

Many of the Comanches who heard Sanco's testimony undoubtedly remembered the mysterious death of Joshua Givens, a well-known Kiowa. The son of the great warrior and diplomat Satank, Givens became a Presbyterian missionary and worked as an interpreter for the Jerome Commission in 1892. He was charged with deceitfully obtaining Indian signatures to the agreement setting terms for allotment and opening lands to whites. Some Indians who opposed the agreement sought revenge. According to tribal tradition, a Kiowa or Comanche medicine man made an effigy of Givens and "made medicine" against him. Givens was told he would become ill, hemorrhage, and die. He died shortly thereafter. The agent listed consumption as the official cause of death, but many Kiowas were convinced it was divine retribution. Missionaries sought to counter the belief that Givens had been struck down because he failed to follow the words and way of the medicine men. By relating his personal encounter with a medicine man, Sanco hoped to convince his listeners that the power of the Christian's God was stronger than the power of the practioners of "evil medicine." However, medicine men continued to have considerable influence among Indians well into the twentieth century.[11]

From the day she arrived at Post Oak, Magdalena Becker participated faithfully and energetically in the life and service of the mission. She was not unfamilar with the hardships and uncertainties of pioneer life, for she had grown up with them on the plains of Kansas and Oklahoma. Nevertheless, her faith and stamina were soon tested in a way she had not experienced before. On August 13, 1902, five months after arriving on the mission field, Magdelena gave birth to their third child, a daughter Augusta. The baby died two days later. In spite of this, the Beckers courageously informed delegates to the General Conference that they remained "very happy in the work of the Lord on the mission field."[12]

In 1903 the Foreign Mission Board approved a request from Magdalena to work half-time as a field matron in the Indian Service. The field matron position was first authorized by the U.S. Congress in 1891. Several missionary wives, including Anna Deyo, were employed in this role, training Indian women in basic homemaking and health skills, and keeping certain tribal records. Having access to the homes of the Indians, Magdalena believed, would serve to create better understanding, improve their quality of life, and promote the spiritual work of the mission. Because of the birth on August 7, 1903 of a son, Peter, and the needs of her young family, Magdalena did not submit her application to the Indian Service until August, 1904. In a letter to agent James F. Randlett, she stated: "There has nothing been done for our Indians west of Cache where our Mennonite Brethren Mission is located. While they are far from school (Ft. Sill) these Ind. have not the advantages that those have close by; therefore they are far behind in everything."[13] Anna Deyo supported Becker's application, writing: "She is an earnest, conscientious woman. Is helpful to the Indians near her and has a sincere desire to help them to a better life, and more, I think she loves them." [14] On December 15,

1904 Mrs. Becker was affirmed (not sworn, for religious reasons) into the office of assistant field matron for the Comanches, West Cache District. Her salary was $25 a month.[15]

Field matrons were required to submit monthly, quarterly, and annual reports. During one period, weekly reports were required. A review of Magdalena Becker's reports during her twenty-eight-year tenure as field matron reveals much information about the social and economic conditions of the Comanche people, and the pace of acculturation during the first three decades of the twentieth century. Her reports also reveal an overriding concern for the welfare of Native Americans. In the early years she traveled an average of more than a hundred miles each month by buggy, was exposed almost daily to communicable diseases, and faced the perils of Oklahoma's changeable and frequently violent weather. Bad roads, often muddy or near non-existent, made travel difficult.

In later years Mrs. Becker traveled as many as 3000 miles annually, mostly by buggy. Her job, in essence, became an extension of the missionary program at Post Oak. Federal Indian policy at that time was based on the theory that civilization and Christianization went hand in hand. It was believed that only after "heathenish" religious ceremonials and beliefs were destroyed, and replaced by the white man's religion and culture, could the Indian become truly civilized.[16] Field matrons were encouraged to propagate Christian beliefs and practices and promote church attendance. In her first home visits as matron, Becker distributed calendars and explained "which days to keep holy and which to work." There was no wall of separation between church and state in Comanche country.[17] Magdalena Becker's missionary work at Post Oak, including Sunday services, were regularly included in her field matron reports.

A gender affinity developed between Magdalena Becker and the Indian women. In her first monthly report, she recorded that "where ever women chopped wood I told men in loving words they should do it. Ind. women felt pleased." Her good rapport with Comanche women was aided by the fact that she quickly learned their language, an accomplishment few other matrons could claim. English was a second language for the Beckers; most of their formal education had been in German. Plautdietsch, a Low German dialect, was spoken in the homes of most Mennonites from Russia, while High German was the language of the church. The Beckers' reports to the Foreign Mission Board were written in German until the 1930s. Mrs. Becker had some difficulty composing reports in English, but her skills improved somewhat with practice.

Becker's first annual report is a comprehensive description of her first eight months as field matron. It gives a good picture of the nature of her work, the type of situations she confronted, and how she dealt with them. Her Mennonite upbringing can be seen in the emphasis on cleanliness, caring for the sick, and providing training in sewing, quilting, and cooking—skills all Mennonite girls learned early in life. The positive tone of this report is typical of the hundreds of reports she filed over the years.

Her annual field matron report for 1905, edited only for brevity, follows:

"Dec 15th 1904 I started in this work as assistent field matron. I have occupied 69 1/2 days in visiting Indian women in there homes and 40 days where I worked at home; had sewing meetings, funerals, campt meeting and nursed a sick Indian.

There are about 70 families in my District. Repeatingly I visited 223 families and 619 persons. About half of the Indians live in houses and the others in tents.

1. Instructed and helped 162 Ind. women in different ways, as follows. Some how to keep house clean, helped to clean windows at several homes, cleaned 6 cupboards, blackened 4 stoves, scrubbed 6 floors and helped to put up shelfs and water stands ect.

2. In Hygienic condition: taught them not to go bare-footed in winter time, not to over heat rooms, which they generally do and causes them to catch cold. Also keep body clean, to get rid of lice. Gave away 15 fine combs. At one place told them how well could be cleaned. Gave reciept for killing bedbugs and in many other ways to enourmous to mention.

3. Taught and showed several how to bake bread, how to cook potatoes, make beef gravy ect. Prepared suitable meals for 8 sick.

4. 52 Garments were made of which some were made while I visited them in there homes and some when they came to my home; and some I made for those that had no sewing machine; also for blind and orphans. . . . Gave away pieces for 41 quilts for Ind. women to piece. Pieces for 20 quilts and 60 pin cushions where cut out on the day of Sewing meeting. . . .

5. At homes told them to wash dirty clothes; clean bed

clothes, which had been used by sick persons.

6. . . . Gave away shelf and crepe paper and rose seeds to decorate rooms to those living in houses.

7. So far I could not interest them on Dairy work or keeping Poultry as they visit and camp out to much.

8. I visited 38 sick some of them several times. Tryed to help them in home treatment such as salve for sores, cough syrup, pergitive medicine and what to wear and eat. Taught several young mothers how to take care after confinement and of a new born child. For 18 days I had to nurse a sick Indian boy named Clarence Lostwolf the son of Chief Crockednose of Daring Montanna, Cheyenne River. . . . He . . . took sick on Typhoid fever. He had no friends to take care of him, So I took him to my home where a Docter from Cache treated him. I waited on him day and night from the 22nd of July to Aug 8th when his Spirit passed to Eternity. He died with penetration of the bowels.

9. I especially instructed young mothers to keep children clean, at some places washed and combed little children. I also visited the school children and often sang songs with them.

10. We had religious Service each Sunday forenoon about 287 persons stayed for dinner we furnished bread and coffee and what more they wanted I asked them to bring it along to be prepared in the camp house, which was espically made for the Indians. Here they had chanches to learn in different ways; I had them at work at every meal.

We had 10 funerals I trimmed 9 coffins; only 1 corpse was laid in a ready made coffin.

There was 1 camp meeting held at this Mission which lasted 2 days.

During these 8 months I traveled 893 miles visiting Indian women in there homes. When I first started in this work I had very much trouble to get them interested; but now have so many volenteer calls that I sometimes cannot attend to them all.

I must say I enjoy the work and find homes more attractive. I find most of them doing as I instructed them.

The average attendance in church is 5 times as large, since this work among the Indian women has been started. . . ." 18

In her January 1906 report Becker mentions, for the first time, a new service, one for which she is remembered to this day: naming newborn babies.[19] Why she took on this responsibility is not clear, but a large number of Comanches born in the Cache-Indiahoma area before 1933 owe their given names to Mrs. Becker. Prior to their reservation days the Comanches had no surnames. Formal or real names were bestowed by a parent or an invited person of distinction. Names might be derived from some closely connected event or be expressive of the parents' pride. Often a child was named after a close relative. Quanah adopted his white mother's name (Parker) after his arrival on the reservation. Nicknames were freely applied and might be used more frequently than the formal name.[20] Missionaries considered it a badge of acceptance and honor to be given an "Indian name."

As part of the government's program to "Americanize" the first Americans, Indians were encouraged to adopt the practice of using both family names and Christian, or given, names. Magdalena Becker apparently agreed with that philosophy. According to a longtime member of the Indiahoma Mennonite Brethren Church, "Mrs. Becker named nearly all of us. She liked short names like Lizzie, the one she gave me."[21] Among the other names she assigned to Indian babies were the following: Russel, Lottie, Esther, Lee, Gilbert, Rhoda, Annie, Linda, Florence, Juanita, Troy, Don, Edith, and Eli. One of the Niedo boys was honored with the name Menno, after Menno Simons, the sixteenth century founder of the Mennonite church.[22] Glenn, the youngest Becker child, recalled that his mother "gave all kinds of names to Indian children, but when I was born she couldn't come up with a name for me. For two to three months they just called me 'Boy.'"[23]

The evil effects of gambling on Indian families became a major concern for the field matron in 1906, and for many years after. Gambling on card games was prevalent whenever lease payments were distributed at the subagency near the Little Red Store at Cache. Many people would stay away from their homes for a month at a time, neglecting their field work and normal home life. Anna Deyo reported in October 1906 that "Mrs. Becker and I are trying to make sewing as popular as gambling at Cache sub-agency, but as yet have not succeeded. We are hoping for better things."[24]

Mrs. Becker assisted with thirteen funerals in 1906, including a service for "the little son of Quanah Parker." His was the only one for whom she and her husband did not need to make the coffin. The field matron's weekday contacts apparently paid off at Post Oak on

Sundays; attendance at the mission in 1906 increased twenty-five percent over the previous year. One can sense her feeling of pride as she
evaluated the year's work: "I must say good results have been obtained.
. . . The women are more interested in there [sic] house work then
before, they keep the children cleaner and it is encouraging to see how
some dress there [sic]children nice and bring them to church."[25]

The year 1907 marked a transition and change for Post Oak
Mission. As the missionary enterprise approached its twelfth year
without any baptized Indian members, the Foreign Mission Board
faced some hard decisions. The Mennonite Brethren Conference
had sent several missionaries to India since 1899 and were continuing
to expand that work.[26] With increased expenditures, some board
members were questioning the cost of maintaining five workers
on a field in Oklahoma that had borne virtually no fruit. Kohfeld's
salary was $700 a year, while Becker received $400. Some felt
staff could be scaled back since three other denominations were
laboring among the Comanches. In fall 1906 Kohfeld and Becker
wrote the mission board that they believed one missionary couple
was sufficient for the field, and that Becker was willing to resign.
Delegates to the General Conference of 1906 voted that only one
missionary couple be employed at Post Oak in the future and that
the mission board be authorized to decide which couple would be
retained.[27]

It appears the board actually considered withdrawing both missionary couples and turning the station over to the American Baptists. According to David C. Peters, members of the Foreign Mission
Board met with E. C. Deyo to discuss whether the Baptists would be
interested in acquiring Post Oak. Deyo reportedly stated that they
would consider doing so, but only if A. J. and Magdalena Becker
would agree to stay on as missionaries. He recommended that the
Mennonite board put the Beckers in charge and continue the mission
effort. Following their conference with Deyo, the board decided to
release the Kohfelds and retain the Beckers for the time being. The
counsel of Rev. Abraham Richert, board member from Korn, apparently decided the issue. He reasoned that the mission land with its
three buildings was debt-free, and that they must have an excellent
missionary couple in the Beckers because the Baptists were eager to
have them.[28]

The mission board's explanation for the "resignation" of Kohfeld
focused on their concern for the health of his wife Elizabeth. Although
it may have been a factor in the board's decision, that was not the

crucial issue. The fact that Mrs. Becker was receiving a salary of $300 a year as assistant field matron, while still able to actively serve at the mission, was a major consideration. J. F. Harms stated that with A. J. Becker and his "strong, energetic wife," they got two missionaries for the price of one. And they believed that Becker was the right man for the job at that time.[29]

Henry Kohfeld found it difficult to accept the board's decision. His 1894 call to be a missionary to the Indians had been so clear to him, he had willingly changed careers to obey it. David C. Peters recalled that he received a letter in which Kohfeld charged that, "I, with the Beckers [had forced] him away from the mission." Peters denied the accusation.[30] Although Kohfeld did not want to leave Post Oak, he ultimately accepted his release as "God's will." He relinquished responsibility for the mission late in 1906, and departed Post Oak in March 1907. He and his family lived in Gotebo, Oklahoma for three years and then moved to Shafter, California where he was active in local Mennonite Brethren churches. He died in 1932, one year after the death of his wife Elizabeth.[31]

When Henry Kohfeld, the Mennonite Brethren Conference of North America's first missionary, left Post Oak, the mission was still on a shaky foundation. His tenure was not without some important achievements, however. Through his persistent efforts, with virtually no help from the Indian agents, he had secured a site from Quanah Parker for a mission station. The first two buildings were constructed under his supervision, and an excellent water supply was obtained. His home visitation ministry won friends, if not converts, for the mission. Home visits would become an important mission strategy under the Beckers. He established the Post Oak Mission Cemetery and helped change the burial customs of Comanches in that area. The annual Christmas program and serving of meals on the station grounds were begun during his time.

Perhaps his greatest contribution was gaining the respect of Chief Quanah Parker. Once Quanah put his stamp of approval on Kohfeld and the work of the mission, as he did at Harold Parker's funeral, the opportunities for progress were greatly enhanced. Still, Kohfeld seemed unable to take advantage of the door opened by Quanah, or the increased attendance stimulated by Mrs. Becker's work as field matron. In twelve years he failed to establish a native church.

It should be noted that slow and sparse results were typical of many pioneer mission endeavors among American Indians. It was only after eight years of ministry that the General Conference

Mennonite Church missionaries baptized their first Indian convert in Oklahoma, and many more years before they established an Indian church.[32] After two years of perseverance the Deyo, or First Comanche Mission, baptized its first convert in 1895, but gained no additional converts until two years later. Once the breakthough occurred, Deyo experienced more success, as was eventually the case at Post Oak under the Beckers.[33] The Beckers consistently praised the Kohfelds for their pioneering work under difficult conditions on the Oklahoma frontier. The Kohfelds planted the seed, they said, that produced the fruit they were privileged to harvest.

Building an Indian Church and Community

Initially, the Beckers agreed to accept a six-month appointment as head missionaries. Only two things, they said, would convince them that God wanted them to stay longer. Firstly, an interpreter who would work with Rev. Becker on a regular basis had to be found; secondly, they needed Indian converts to organize a church. "We asked God for two things, souls and an interpreter," Mrs. Becker reported. The outcome would determine their future. "We would either win or lose out."[1]

The first Sunday after the Kohfelds' departure, the Beckers were surprised to see a young government interpreter, Herman Asenap (Greyfoot), enter the church before the start of services. They were even more surprised when the Comanche told Rev. Becker he would be willing to interpret for him whenever needed. He had previously declined to serve in that capacity, but now he said, "You and your wife have been so kind to me. Last night I could not sleep. So now I want to interpret for you, and I want no money." With tears streaming down his face, Becker embraced him and said, "You're an answer to my prayers."[2]

Now the stage was set for a pivotal event that would literally determine the fate of Post Oak Mission. Having pledged "to work hard for six months" to win converts, Rev. Becker decided to hold extended tent meetings near Red Store while the Indians camped there to collect and spend their cash disbursements. Leaving their three small children with a housekeeper, the Beckers packed their camping equipment and supplies and joined an Indian encampment just outside of Cache. Approximately 500 Indians were camped near the subagency and trading post. The Beckers pitched their own tent and a bigger one for gospel meetings near a spacious tent used for dancing, gambling, and other entertainment. Every evening the missionary proclaimed the gospel through his interpreter, Herman Asenap, who showed up regularly and promptly to assist.

While her husband called on families during the day, Magdalena spent time sewing with Indian women and improving her Comanche language skills. Although a number of people came each night to hear the white missionaries sing and preach, two weeks went by without any positve response to the message. Lonesome for her children,

weary of cooking meals over a campfire on the cold prairie, and physi-
cally drained, Magdalena confessed that her "heart was about to break."
Deeply discouraged, she walked to a nearby stand of timber where
she broke down and cried like "a wild Indian."

A woman named Wi-e-puh saw Mrs. Becker sobbing. She placed
her arms around her and asked, "Why do you cry so?" Mrs. Becker
replied, "I would not care about how we suffer, but your Indian people are tramping my God with their feet, they do not want to be
saved." Wi-e-puh made no response at the time; however, that evening
during the tent service she walked to the front bench and committed
herself to the "Jesus Way." Six others, including one man, soon followed her example. With the baptism of these first converts, a
Comanche Mennonite Brethren Church was born.[3] As a result of
this success, the practice of conducting protracted meetings at camp
gatherings became one of Becker's main mission strategies.

This spiritual breakthrough was fraught with religious symbol-
ism, for one of the converts was named Her-wa-nee, meaning "dawn
of day." This truly was the dawn of a new day for Post Oak Mission.
From then on not a year would pass, while the Beckers were missionaries, without the addition of new converts to the mission rolls. When
a daughter was born to the Beckers on December 14, 1907, they
named her Herwanna, a continuing reminder of the significant events
of that year. Those events launched the young couple on lengthy
careers working with the Comanches of Oklahoma.

Sam Mo-Wat (No Hand), baptized on July 21, 1907, became
the first Indian member of the Post Oak Mission Church. He received the name No Hand as a boy of six when he tried to rescue a pet
bear cub that had fallen from a lodge pole into a pot of boiling water.
His fingers never developed normally and he was left with a badly
deformed hand.[4] Nevertheless, he mastered the art of shooting buffalos with a bow and arrow and participated in tribal warfare. For a
short time he worked as a cowboy on the Burnett Ranch in Texas,
where he acquired the name Sam. He frequently told the story of
how a whip snake dropped from an overhanging limb and wrapped
itself around his neck. He finally managed to slip part of the snake
over his chin and into his mouth. Biting with all the strength in his
jaws he broke the snake's backbone and freed himself.

No Hand exhibited a curiosity about the Mennonite mission
early on, but for years scorned the idea of taking the "Jesus Road."
Once converted, he retained his Christian commitment until his death
in 1953 at age 90. Yet he never lost his unique Comanche identity.

He wore his hair in long braids until later in life and never abandoned his native tongue, learning very little English. He demonstrated that it was possible to become a Christian and still be a Comanche, an important lesson for the missionaries and his fellow tribespeople. His wife Cheek-sa also became a member of the church in the early years.[5] No Hand served as an usher for many years. This uninhibited and free-spirited man did not hesitate to interrupt services to forcibly eject any dog unfortunate enough to stray into the "Jesus House." Since he suffered from diminished hearing, he did not realize how loud his shouts and the dog's yelps were as he chased out the unwelcome intruder.[6] He was an excellent silversmith and craftsman, and gave prized gifts of bracelets and bows and arrows to missionary children.[7]

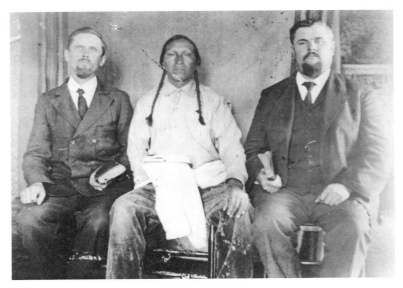

Rev. A. J. Becker (White Beard), Mo-Wat (No Hand), first baptized convert at Post Oak Mission, and Rev. M.M. Just (Big Chief), Mennonite Brethren minister
Credit: Archives & Manuscripts Division of the Oklahoma Historical Society

No Hand was an avid story teller. He enjoyed recounting tribal myths and legends and passing on the old Comanche ways to the younger generation. Herwanna Becker Barnard included some of his stories in a master's thesis at the University of Oklahoma. She stated that No Hand would spend hours telling his grandchildren bedtime stories. He would imitate the sounds of animals, birds, waterfalls, horse hoofs, thunder, and lightning, and mimic the actions of characters in the stories. This song, translated from the Comanche, was composed by No Hand for use at the mission:

> "Jesus, my Savior, I am telling the story, I am telling the story.
> Down here on this earth, The Word must be given.
> I am telling the story, I am telling the story,
>   I am telling the story.
> Up there in Heaven, Where all appears wonderful,
> We will be made whole again.
> I am telling the story, I am telling the story,
>   I am telling the story."[8]

No Hand proved to be a mainstay of Post Oak Mission.

Another person of critical importance to the eventual success of Post Oak was Herman Asenap, the interpreter. In his upper teens when he volunteered to become Becker's regular interpreter, this remarkable man continued in that service until his death in 1960. The first generation of Christian converts at Post Oak received their spiritual birth and nurture from the "Gospel According to Herman," even though he himself did not become a baptized believer until 1932. His father, a Mexican, had been taken captive by Comanches at a young age and absorbed into the tribe. He was given the name Asenap, meaning "grey foot," by a tribal elder who saw him and his soon-to-be bride emerge from a creek bed with clay mud on their feet. Eventually he became a great and feared medicine man.

Herman had an eighth grade education, unusual for Indians or whites at that time, worked in a bank, and served as an interpreter for the Indian Office. On at least one occasion he traveled to Washington to help conduct tribal business. In 1933 he was one of two "indispensable interpreters and go-betweens" for the Santa Fe Laboratory of Anthropology group that conducted a field study of Comanche culture in Oklahoma.[9] His first wife was Two-Va-Bitty, with whom he had five children. After her death he married Bessie Parker, the daughter of Quanah Parker. They had four children. A granddaughter, Arlene Asenap, stated that her grandfather insisted on getting his children and grandchildren involved in the church services "by making them sing or learn verses from the Bible to say in front of the church." To this day this practice is followed by little children in the Indiahoma Mennonite Brethren Church. Another recollection by the granddaughter typifies the deep commitment of Herman Asenap:

"When his eyesight began to fail in later years he would learn the scripture by heart so he could ·pretend he was reading it; at times he couldn't see the printed page but he wanted to do his job."[10]

A. J. Becker came to realize that the Comanches were more open to the gospel when they heard it in their own language. Although he gained competency at a conversational level, he found it difficult to explain scriptural truths and theological concepts in the Comanche tongue. To translate his German "thinking" into English was diffficult enough; turning it into comprehensible Comanche was even more problematic. Using a capable interpreter was the next best option, and in Herman Asenap he had one of the best. Becker's heavy reliance on Asenap may have hindered his attainment of fluency in the language. Failure to achieve mastery of Comanche was

Herman Asenap and A.J. Becker, 1927. Asenap was the first Comanche interpreter at Post Oak and served in that position from 1907 until the end of the mission period.
Credit: Cornelius Wall photo, Center for Mennonite Brethren Studies, Hillsboro KS.

undoubtedly a limiting factor in his early ministry. Magdalena Becker, on the other hand, worked hard and successfully to achieve fluency in the native tongue, which greatly enhanced her effectiveness as a field matron.

It is doubtful that Rev. Becker's adherence to the English language in religious services was influenced by government policy. In its concerted efforts to acculturate tribal Americans, the government sought every means possible to suppress native cultures and languages. School children, for example, were severely punished if discovered speaking in their native dialects.[11] Becker clearly understood the efficacy of communicating religious teachings in the language of the people. His own family, and thousands of his co-religionists, had left Russia in the mid-1870s, in part because of threatened restrictions on their German language. After thirty-five years in North America, all Mennonite Brethren churches still used only the German language in their religious services. In 1915 Becker wrote that he was considering leaving the mission field because, "We are German and desire that our children remain German."[12] He also retained D. C. Peters for a while in his home to tutor his children in German. As it turned out, only the older Becker children continued to use German, for there were few opportunities to utilize it. But they all learned Comanche.

Comanche language usage among the younger generation of Indians declined rapidly during the 1940s, and particularly after World War II. Becker continued to conduct bilingual services until his retirement. Other area missionaries also relied extensively on interpreters.

Before their self-imposed six-month trial period as missionaries had ended, the Beckers' prayers had been answered: they had an interpreter and Indian converts. At the Mennonite Brethren General Conference, November 10-12, 1907, held in Dalmeny, Saskatchewan, Canada, the mission board informed the delegates it had released Kohfeld from the field and appointed Becker as head missionary. It was noted, "The brethren Kohfeld and Becker could part wishing each other blessing." The board reported that within the last few months Becker had baptized seven converts, resulting in the birth of an Indian Mennonite Brethren Church.[13] After twelve years this was good news indeed for the Mennonite Brethren Conference. The delegates authorized the ordination of Becker by his home church at Isabella, Oklahoma.

According to the Church Roll and Record Book listing members of Post Oak Mission, the first seven Indian church members and the dates of baptism were: Sam Mow wat (Nohand), July 21, 1907; Wieper (Mary Koweno), August 18, 1907; Chock suh, August 18, 1907; Totite Heath, September 22, 1907; Corine Heath (Washe), September 22, 1907; Herwaney (Chewaheh), September 29, 1907; and Cassie Heath, October 27, 1907 (Names are spelled as shown in the Record Book).[14] Based on oral history, the first seven baptized converts were: Mo-Wat (No Hand); Wi-e-puh, the first woman convert and the wife of "Deacon" George Koweno; Her-wa-nee; To-tie; O-Sa-kena; Ni-ve-wah; and Nuna-to-vetsuh.[15] (Listed as currently spelled.)

Other changes affected Post Oak Mission in 1907. On November 16, Oklahoma was admitted as the forty-sixth state in the Union. Five months earlier a fee simple patent, giving title to the approximately 158 acres of land on which the mission stood, was granted to the "American Mennonite Brethren Mission Union," the entity incorporated to transact legal matters for the mission board. The document, signed by President Theodore Roosevelt, was endorsed by M. M. Just and Peter Wiens for the "Mission Union," and by A. J. Becker as "Station Missionary."[16]

Becker assumed jurisdiction over a mission field of about three hundred Indians, living in seventy to seventy-five families. Situated in western Comanche County, the field was roughly twenty-five miles long by twelve miles wide. There were three other denominations working among the approximately 1,400 Comanches living on their allotments in Comanche, Cotton, and Caddo counties. The various religious groups had informally agreed to set boundaries for their fields to avoid possible conflict. Most of the Indians in the Post Oak area were members of the Quahada (Antelope) bands. The other four major Comanche divisions were the Penatekas (Wasps), Noconis (Wanderers), Yamparikas (Root Eaters), and Kotsatekas (Buffalo Eaters). The American Baptist's First Comanche Mission, generally called the Deyo Mission, was located five miles east and two south of Cache; the Methodist and Dutch Reformed missions were near Lawton. There were also several denominations working among the Kiowas in the northern part of the reservation.

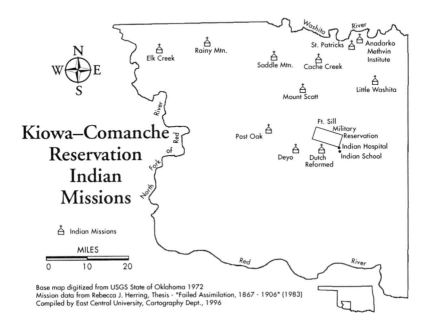

Kiowa–Comanche
Reservation
Indian
Missions

Base map digitized from USGS State of Oklahoma 1972
Mission data from Rebecca J. Herring, Thesis - "Failed Assimilation, 1867 - 1906" (1983)
Compiled by East Central University, Cartography Dept., 1996

Some of the missionaries gained a reputation for exhibiting "an unholy interest in land." J. J. Methvin acquired 160 acres for a Methodist mission near Anadarko. Within a few years he had managed to obtain over 280 acres of additional land for substations at Mount Scott, Little Washita, and Ware's Chapel. When he set his eyes on a quarter section of excellent farming land to further expand his program, the Indian agent, unimpressed, managed to stop the project. W. W. Carithers managed to obtain 640 acres to operate a Reformed Presbyterian mission and school. When he tried to have his former students' allotments located nearby, he ran into conflict with cattlemen who held leases in the area. His pursuit of land also raised the ire of some Indians. A Comanche who was offered $100 for his land told Carithers he would not sell to him even if he gave him enough money to fill his tepee up to the smoke hole.

E. C. Deyo was not only interested in evangelizing Indians; he also promoted the opening of reservation lands to non-Indians. He wrote "boomer" articles for the Marlow newspaper, extolling in hyperbolic terms the well-watered "broad green prairies" and rich mineral deposits waiting for development by "industrious Christian whites." This kind of activity, and the land hunger exhibited by some churchmen, may explain the cool reception Comanches and Kiowas gave the early missionaries. It also provides fodder for the critics of Christian missionaries sent by religious bodies to presumably uplift and improve the Indian tribes.[17]

The Kiowa-Comanche-Apache agency was located at Anadarko, fifty-eight miles from Post Oak, and five subagencies were scattered across the territory. Post Oak's nearest subagency was at Cache. District farmers and two or three field matrons were assigned to provide services for the Comanches. Indian schools were located at Anadarko and Fort Sill; later an Indian hospital would be established near Lawton. There was only one physician serving the Kiowa agency.

For many years after their settlement on the reservation the Comanches received rations. By the time the Beckers arrived at Post Oak this system was being phased out, but the Indians continued to receive per capita payments derived from grassland leases and interest on tribal funds held in the United States Treasury. Distributed several times a year, the payments ranged from thirty to sixty dollars per person. Field matrons often helped distribute the payments. Most adults also received money from land leases, choosing to rent their allotments rather than work them, retaining only a few acres on which to reside. From the various sources, the average Comanche family received an income of $400 to $500 a year, barely enough to eke out a precarious existence.[18]

A breakthrough in establishing a mission church had occurred in 1907; nevertheless, progress for some time after was still slow, and the work often discouraging. Nine new members were added in 1908, but there were only three in the following year. "The work last year [1909] was very difficult, but not only on our field," Becker reported. He stated that only one Indian had been baptized at the Kiowa Rainy Mountain Mission and only three at Deyo Mission. He blamed whites for contributing to the problem. "The white man spurs the native Indians to all sorts of amusements. An Indian has little will power to resist. Drinks are offered, almost forced upon them. In this way the Indian becomes more apathetic toward the gospel, which the soul really longs for." Becker believed that Indians by and large, however, "worldly as they may be, still have religious inclinations, and they have a general longing to be saved." Becker noted another problem—peyote worship. Indians could not comprehend why their religion should not be sufficient for them to be saved, since they prayed to the same God. They failed to understand, he said, that they must come to God "through Christ," and that they "cannot come to Him through the mescal [peyote] bean." He found this concept difficult to explain to the Native Americans.[19]

Many Comanches found the "Jesus Road" as mapped by the Mennonite Brethren extremely narrow and difficult to traverse. The rules against dancing and playing cards were particularly onerous. Tribal dancers were in growing demand at public functions and such activity could provide a much needed income for participants. Card playing was a major pastime, with or without gambling; either way it was considered a sin precluding church membership. One woman who came to Rev. Becker for baptism claimed she had been converted six years earlier, but had not been willing to give up playing cards until now. A number of Indians were refused baptism because, according to Becker, "they had not been saved from their heathenish ways. What would it profit if their names are put on the church rolls but are not written in heaven?"[20]

Seven persons were added to the church in 1910, bringing the total membership to twenty-three, of whom nineteen were Indians. "It's only one soul at a time," Becker wrote the *Zionsbote*, "but we are thankful for that."[21] He was also grateful for other small but promising signs of acculturation. Together with mission board members M. M. Just and Peter Wiens, he had visited the home of George and

Mary (Wi-e-puh) Koweno, two early converts. They found this Indian couple to be model housekeepers and proficient small-scale farmers. With ten acres of corn and a large garden under cultivation, the husband "had worked more in one year than in his whole life previously," Becker boasted. They were doing as well "as the best whites."[22] Indian culture would not die out, he predicted, but it would change. "More and more they are taking on our culture, in clothing, food, work, etc."[23] Furthermore, he found the religious devotion of his converts truly impressive. When the old man Na-pay was converted on New Year's Day, 1912, he insisted on being baptized immediately, even though it required breaking the ice on the baptismal pond. A Comanche woman named Botsis gave birth to a son on a Saturday and showed up the next day at the mission, having travelled fifteen miles by wagon, because she did not want to miss communion. "When Indians get saved," Becker observed, "then come what may, they're going to church."[24]

Indians had also assumed responsibility for bringing much of the food served at the Sunday mission activities. For many years the missionaries provided all the food. At first the Indians may have come to enjoy the "loaves and fishes" more than the Word of God. But the communal meals, open to those who stayed for the afternoon services, continued to attract people. The direct correlation between the sharing of meals and attendance is not known, but in 1910 Becker reported he had held 140 meetings, some with other missions, with a total attendance of 7,200. Such large turnouts provided the Mennonite missionaries real grounds for optimism.[25]

Wi-e-puh, first Indian convert at Post Oak and her husband George Koweno, the first deacon.
Credit: Courtesy of Marjorie Kelley

The ethnic and racial diversity represented in Sunday services at Post Oak in the early years is noteworthy. A typical congregation would include Comanches, a few Kiowas, Mexicans, blacks, and whites. Conducting the service was a German from Russia whose broken English was translated into the Comanche language. There seems to have been no problem integrating these different groups into the congregation. Blacks living in the vicinity started attending after one of them received medical help from the Beckers for his frozen feet.[26] There were generally good relations between the Mexicans and Indians in this area. A number of Comanches, including the interpreter Herman Asenap and the Hoahwah family, were descendants of Mexican captives who had been absorbed by the tribe.[27]

In 1911 Becker added a ministry to the "Amerikanern" (Americans) living in the vicinity. Separate Sunday afternoon and evening services were held for them for a number of years. Becker made it clear to the mission board that they were not neglecting the Indians by taking on this added responsibility. Some neighboring missionaries reduced their services to Indians in order to accomodate the white population. Conducting five services per Sunday apparently proved too tiring for the Beckers and the separate services for whites were eventually dropped.[28] By the end of 1915, a total of seventy-eight persons–forty-eight or forty-nine Indians, ten or eleven Mexicans, and nineteen whites–

Mrs. Becker, first row on the right, with a group of women at Post Oak Mission. Back row on left is Maddische who lived to age 110.   Credit: The Center for Mennonite Brethren Studies, Fresno CA

had become members of the church. A number of these, including at least seven Indians, had died by that date and others had moved away. Two members had been excommunicated "because of the sin of fornication that found its sneaking way into those two lives." [29]

Home visitation was an important aspect of Rev. Becker's ministry. It was a way to establish personal relationships that fostered trust and understanding, which he considered essential in working with Native Americans. By 1915 he was averaging between two to three hundred home visits per year.[30] The Comanches enjoyed visiting with the jovial, sociable White Beard, as they fondly called their blond-bearded missionary. Often he arrived with his pockets filled with candy for the little children. Many of his calls were to minister spiritually to the sick; the Indians were plagued with serious health problems. Tuberculosis, smallpox, and typhoid epidemics were common at the turn of the century and the death rate was high, especially among infants. During the smallpox siege of 1901-1902, forty-two Indians had been buried at Post Oak cemetery. More and more Indians were turning to missionary Becker for help in their times of sickness and death. In some years, hardly a month passed when he did not conduct at least one funeral. In 1913 he buried twenty-three, and by 1915 there were 138 graves in Post Oak Cemetery.[31]

The missionaries maintained that the Indians relied too much on medicine men, resorting to white doctors only after it was too late, if at all. Since there was only one government physician with the Indian agency, it is perhaps not surprising that medicine men continued to flourish. Mrs. Becker tried for years to get the Indian Service to provide a government physician for the West Cache District, but to no avail. It was difficult to persuade tribespeople to go to the Indian hospital at Lawton or to see local private doctors. One Comanche complained to Rev. Becker that "all white doctor do to us is say `stick out tongue, stick back in, three dollars, please.'"[32]

Many Indians chose to bring their sick to the mission station for treatment by "Mother Becker." They might camp on the grounds for several days, or even weeks. During one period in 1912-13, there were sick Indians camped on the Becker yard for thirty-six consecutive days. In the third quarter of 1914 Magdalena attended to six persons, two with typhoid fever, for nearly two months. Not only did she serve as a general nurse and administer medications, she also prepared special meals for them. As if that were not enough, her five children and husband also contracted typhoid, forcing her to take leave from her job to care for them. "It was work day and night . . .

Magdalena Becker on the right with a group of Comanche children and three early day members of Post Oak Mission. The "Death House", an addition to the church where the deceased were prepared for burial, is shown on the back right.
Credit: Courtesy of Marjorie Kelley

and hard for me," she confessed. But she could report that her family and all but one of the patients recovered.

The agency superintendent recommended Mrs. Becker be granted paid leave time to nurse her family back to health. Her devoted care for the Indian patients camped on her yard had undoubtedly caused her family's illness, he wrote. The Indian Office agreed that Becker had demonstrated conspicuous dedication and fortitude but refused to approve pay for the leave time taken. Despite this ordeal, and the lack of appreciation by her superiors in Washington, no sick Indians were ever turned away by the Beckers, much to the amazement of the Indian agents. The Indian Office provided the field matrons with some medical supplies and Dr. J. Allen Perisho, physician at Cache, gave the Beckers assistance when called.[33]

Indians also brought their dead to the Becker home to be buried. An addition to the church building, called the "Death House," served as morgue. For many years Rev. Becker made the coffins, gravestones, and vaults for Indian burials. The Becker children recalled being awakened many nights by Indians bringing in a family member who had died. Rev. Becker observed that "Indians never hurried about everyday things that came up in their lives, but when one of them died, they couldn't hurry fast enough to get him buried." He remembered one incident where a group of Indians rushed up to their house with a body and announced they wanted "old man Ki-yah" buried at once. The Beckers quickly made a coffin and trimmed it with black and white cloth. When all was ready, they discovered the Indian "really wasn't dead yet." He did not die until two days later. Since this was in the days before they had the "Death House," and his wife refused to go to bed "with that casket in the room," Becker hid the coffin under the bed until the man died. On another occasion, during a very cold night, a baby said to be dead was brought to the house. According to Rev. Becker, "It was wrapped up very good and thinking it was dead, we left it on the porch that night. The next morning we opened the bundle and the baby wasn't dead." The mother left the infant girl in Mrs. Becker's care, but she died a few days later. Rev. Becker wrote," My wife and I both cried."[34]

The Beckers built a small beautifully lined wooden casket and arranged a memorial service for the child. The sounds of loud wailing signaled the arrival at Post Oak of the baby's grieving relatives. Inside the mission chapel, Rev. Becker gently and emotionally spoke words of comfort repeated by the interpreter despite his own choking tears. As the line to view the body formed, the chanting and wailing resumed, growing louder and more intense. Overcome by grief, the girl's mother fainted and crumpled to the ground. A few dashes of cool well water administered by one of the Becker boys revived the woman, but left her dripping wet. Then members of the family went from one mourner to another wiping away their tears, after which the chanting ceased. As the coffin was lowered into the grave, several women removed their beautiful shawls and draped them reverently over the top. Rev. Becker conducted hundreds of funerals during his ministry but he and his family would never forget that particular tragedy.[35]

What frustrated Magdalena the most in her government work was the seeming gambling addiction of many Indians. She saw this as a major impediment to the progress she believed was beginning to be made in the civilization program. On March 19, 1908 she wrote the Indian agent at Anadarko that she was at her wit's end and needed advice. She had been trying to make her rounds but found practically no one at home. Since the latest lease payments the Indians in her district had been gambling "every day in the week, also on Sundays and many nights nearly all night." Many who had diligently worked their farms the previous year were not putting in crops this spring. Instead, they had moved closer to West Cache subagency to gamble or watch others gamble. She was anxious to help the women plant spring gardens and assist them with spring housecleaning, but their houses were empty. "I have only the Christians and a few others who are at home to work with." She had managed to get the subagent to order the gambling to stop, but the Indians refused to comply, insisting that they had a right to gamble. Since she could not fulfill her duties as matron, she concluded, "I thought to let you know how things are."[36]

The gambling problem finally prompted the government to make some changes. The per capita payment schedule was changed so the Indians would receive less money per distribution. This decision was supported by Mrs. Deyo, Mrs. Becker, and other field matrons. Deyo had recommended for years that "the Comanches should have less money and more work."[37] Becker called the new policy a "wise plan" since "these big payments have been a curse to most of the Comanches here, who will not work but Gamble as regular as we eat our meals." She had observed the Comanches for nine years, she said, "and I have found that most of them will not work as long as they have money but will squander it away for nonsense." She believed that if the money payments were stopped it would do them good, "help to civilize them," and make her work "more productive." But she had one misgiving: "I would be sorrow [sic] if the money would have to be withheld from the good Indians that work and do not Gamble." The "good Indians," she said, "have farmed more this year [1910] than ever before."[38]

The judgemental tone reflected in Mrs. Becker's comments, suggesting the only good Indian is a working Indian, was atypical for her. It revealed her great dismay over the gambling controversy that engulfed the agency. The Comanches were not lazy, but were frustrated with reservation and allotment life. Transforming the Comanches into yeoman farmers was the desired goal, but government officials did not supply them with suitable farming equipment, nor did they consider that Comanche lands often lacked sufficient rainfall for agriculture. Torrential rains were followed by prolonged drought. During one eighteen-month-long dry spell it did not once rain enough to cause water to run in Post Oak Creek. Most of the land in the Wichita Mountains area was better suited for large scale ranching, beyond the Indians' means, than farming. Seventy-five percent of allotments in that area were classified as grazing land.[39] The Comanches, therefore, had few ways to be industrious. As it turned out, Becker's "good," or Christian, Indians were not excluded from the new policy about payments. Sunday offerings at Post Oak Mission declined as a result. The change in the cash payment schedule was only temporary. Subsequently the state of Oklahoma sought to curb gambling by the passage of stronger anti-gambling laws.[40]

Quanah Parker and the Mennonites

Quanah Parker and the Mennonites at Post Oak developed a cordial relationship. The missionaries' interactions with the chief and his family were much more extensive than is generally recognized. A mixed blood who maintained a remarkable blend of progressive and traditional beliefs, Quanah was "the classic middleman, a type appearing among the tribes undergoing the trauma of acculturation under reservation conditions."[1] He made frequent trips to Washington where he became a celebrity. Theodore Roosevelt invited him to participate in his presidential inaugural parade and later visited with him while on a hunting trip in Oklahoma.

Quanah's use of peyote and his many wives must have bothered the Mennonite missionaries, but, based on available records, they never criticized him personally for these practices. Before the Beckers arrived in Oklahoma, the commissioner of Indian affairs informed the chief that he must pick one wife and order the other six to leave. Quanah told the official that he should make the selection, and also be the one to tell the rest to go. He had children by all of his wives except To-nar-cy and loved and cared for them equally.[2] The commissioner backed off and Quanah received little further government harassment. In 1900 the chief had five wives, but within a few years three chose to leave. To-nar-cy and To-pay, the last two wives, remained with him until his death in 1911. To-pay said the wives worked peacefully at family chores and ate at one big table. "It was like a picnic every day."[3] However, the table was not large enough to seat all the wives and children, so they usually ate in shifts.[4]

According to a grandson and Mennonite mission convert, Baldwin (Buster) Parker Jr., Quanah succeeded in running a peaceful and orderly household through organization and good management. "Each morning, grandfather got up early and outlined all the assignments and activities of the day."[5] There were duties for the "upstairs wife," the "downstairs wife," the wife who took care of outdoor chores, and for other helpmates the chief had at any given time.[6] When asked by Grace Hoahwah how it felt to be one of the wives of Quanah Parker, To-pay replied, "It was an honor to be chosen by him."[7]

Quanah Parker's Star House, northwest of Cache and not far from Post Oak Mission.
Credit: Archives & Manuscripts Division of the Oklahoma Historical Society

Anna Hiebert, a longtime volunteer mission worker who first came to Post Oak Mission in 1908, cited one case of an Indian woman with three husbands. They lived together in one camp and got along well. Hiebert said that in the early days she never heard of a husband deserting his wives. An old warrior told her they learned desertion, along with getting drunk, from the whites.[8]

Like other missionaries, the Beckers deplored the use of peyote as a substitute for Christianity or the white man's medicine. Chief Parker appeared at the Oklahoma Constitutional Convention to prevent a proposal to ban peyote, claiming a right to use it as medicine. "We will use the medicine of the white doctors, but we desire to be allowed to use peyote also," he declared. He used peyote in religious ceremonies, but was so circumspect that agent James Randlett claimed no knowledge of Quanah's leadership role in what would come to be known as the Native American Church.[9] The absence of expressions of concern in their reports could indicate that the Beckers also were not aware of Quanah's active participation in the cult.

Quanah's determination that his people adapt to the economic, educational, and political system of the dominant culture could only have been strengthened by his friendship with the Beckers. For many years Magdalena Becker was the only field matron to serve his people in the West Cache district. He saw firsthand the improved standard of living and quality of life for those who cooperated with her visitation program and participated in her classes and at the mission. This kind, selfless, but firm woman was widely loved and respected in the area. Many Comanche women regularly attended weekly training sessions at Post Oak, gaining skills in sewing, quilting, canning, cooking, and crafts. To-pay also attended some of the meetings. She had artistic talent and enjoyed making beautifully shaped flowers from tissue paper to be used to adorn graves in the mission cemetery on Decoration Day. She also made arches that were covered with flowers and placed over the graves. Post Oak gained a reputation as the most beautifully decorated cemetery in the entire Kiowa-Comanche country. To-pay eventually became a baptized member of the Mennonite Brethren Mission Church.[10]

The pacifistic Mennonites may have influenced the chief in another way. According to J. Evetts Haley, Quanah on one occasion stopped the army at Fort Sill from recruiting his band members. "He pointed out that white missionaries were now teaching them that it was wrong to go to war. Therefore, he reasoned, it was inconsistent for the whites to recruit them into an outfit whose sole purpose was fighting."[11] The missionaries were not identified, but it is known that Kohfeld and the Beckers did not hide that they were conscientious objectors to war.

Quanah only occasionally attended religious services at Post Oak Mission, although some of his family members participated more regularly. He was most likely to show up with his large family at special events, such as the Christmas festival, the mission's biggest event. The Mennonite Brethren traditionally handed out free bags of candy to all members and guests. Indians, Christian and non-Christian alike, brought their gifts for family and friends and hung them on a giant Christmas tree or piled them in huge stacks underneath. A generous people, the Comanches enjoyed group festivities and did not think Christmas should be a private family affair. It generally took about two hours to distribute the presents. Contrary to stereotyped images of Indian revelry and holiday drunkenness, Becker recalled that during forty-two years of hosting Christmas gatherings at Post Oak he never witnessed any evidence of drunkenness among the participants.[12]

Quanah Parker selected Post Oak Cemetery as his family burial site, and at least two of his children were interred there before his own death. On December 4, 1910 it also became the reburial location for his beloved mother, Cynthia Ann Parker. For several years Quanah had wanted to remove his mother's grave from near Poyner, Texas to Post Oak Mission. After congress appropriated $1000 to defray the costs, his wish could be carried out. He asked Magdalena Becker to help him arrange a big feast for the occasion. The chief wanted food for about 200 guests, a task not beyond Magdalena's capabilities. Both cultures–Mennonite and Comanche–loved to eat. Food was a major part of social gatherings and no effort was spared in culinary preparations.

Chief Parker selected his mother's plot with his own death in mind. He asked Rev. Becker in which direction the cemetery would be extended. Told it was being built toward the west, he chose a spot on a little knoll east of the existing graves and announced that was where he wanted to be buried also. To Comanches the east, symbol of the rising sun, signifies reviving life. "Like I have been a leader to my people during life," he told Becker, "I want to continue to be their leader after death. For that reason you shall bury me at the head of the Comanches who have died and lie buried here."[13]

Sunday, December 4, in the words of Magdalena Becker, "was a great day for our chief."[14] The day before she had "cooked and baked all day" to prepare for the great event. The chief furnished four beeves and a wagonload of delicacies of every description.[15] A crowd of 700

Quanah Parker, Comanche chief, by the casket of Cynthia Ann Parker in the Post Oak Mission church, December 4, 1910.   Credit: Courtesy of Glenn Becker

people, both Indians and whites, attended the reburial ceremony for Cynthia Ann Parker. Rev. Becker and Rev. E. C. Deyo conducted the service. Quanah also addressed the gathering, first in Comanche and then in English. He said he was happy to bring his mother's body to be buried near his home on the mission grounds. He recalled for his listeners that she "love Indians so well no want to go back to folks." She had never adjusted to white society after her "rescue" from the Comanches and remained grief-stricken until her death in 1870.

According to Daniel Becker, who witnessed the reburial ceremony, the chief urged his people to "follow after white way, get educate, know work, make living when payments stop." He told them they "got to know pick cotton, plow corn." He admonished them to "know white man's God," and said that "when end comes. . . then I want to see my mother again." Sometime during the day, according to Mrs. Becker, he remarked that "perhaps in a year—posssibly ten—I will be lying next to my mother." It turned out he was too optimistic; barely two months later the last chief of the Comanches was dead.[16]

Quanah's health had been failing for some time, reportedly due to complications from asthma and rheumatism. Visiting the Cheyennes at Hammon, Oklahoma, he became critically ill. On the morning of February 25, 1911 the Beckers received a telegram informing them the chief was returning home by train and requesting that they meet him in Indiahoma. Rev. Becker drove his horse full speed to intercept him at the station, but when they got there the train had already left for Cache. By the time they arrived in Cache, Quanah had been taken to the star house by his son-in-law, Emmet Cox. To-Pay asked if he would object to bringing in a white doctor, to which he reportedly replied, "No, it's good. I'm ready." J. Allen Perisho, a physician from Cache, administered a heart stimulant, but to no avail. When it became evident that Quanah was near death, Quas-e-Aye, a medicine man, was called in. He attempted, with an eagle bone, to clear a passage in Quanah's throat so that his wife To-nar-cy might give him medicine. "Parker coughed, gasped, and died," stated a newspaper account. Within twenty minutes of his arrival at home, and before the Beckers could get there, the chief had expired. The missionaries' frantic efforts to reach Parker in time "to administer the medicine of a white man's God" had killed their best horse. When the Beckers arrived they found the chief's family badly shaken. "Three of his daughters fainted," Magdalena wrote. The missionary couple immediately sent messages to inform the Parker children who were not at home.[17]

Since the Comanche custom was to bury the dead as quickly as possible, funeral and burial services were scheduled for the following day at Post Oak Mission. On the morning of February 24 Indian and white relatives and friends gathered at Quanah's Star House to express their grief and pay their respects. Indian superintendent Ernest Stecker represented the government. At twelve-thirty the funeral procession, stretching a mile-and-a-half, started for Post Oak Mission, the body transported in a spring wagon. To-nar-cy, said to be the favorite wife, rode in a car while To-pay and other members of the family—there were at least fifteen surviving children—sat in the bed of a farm wagon. An estimated twelve hundred people attended the services, far more than could crowd into the white frame mission church. "It was the largest crowd that our little mission had ever or will ever see," observed Magdalena Becker.[18]

The services opened with the song, "Tell it to Jesus," sung as a duet by the Beckers. Rev. Deyo, still grieving over the death of his wife ten months earlier, gave the invocation. Following a congregational song sung in Comanche, Rev. Becker addressed the large audience in English, basing his message on Psalm 90. An interpreter, probably Herman Asenap, translated his words into Comanche. Occasionally the interpreter had trouble comprehending statements, so Becker would restate the sentences in an undertone, using different terminology. The Indians—Christian and non-Christian—could probably relate well to the words of the psalmist, "Before the mountains were brought forth, or ever thou hadst formed the earth and the world, even from everlasting to everlasting, thou art God." They could also probably appreciate the allusions to humankind's mortality: "They are like grass which in the morning flourisheth and groweth up; in the evening it is cut down, and withereth." But the words, "The days of our years are three score and ten," probably did not resonate with most of them. Few reservation Indians reached that age. Quanah, it is believed, was fifty-nine. Rev. Becker recalled some of the virtues and progressive ideas of his mixed blood friend, and reminded the Comanches that their chief had urged them at Cynthia Ann Parker's burial to accept his white mother's God.

After the sermon the casket was carried to the grave site, only recently selected by Quanah, and opened for a final viewing. Clothed in his best buckskin suit, Parker was surrounded by feathers, a war bonnet, and Indian relics. While the crowd filed by for a last glimpse of the chief, the missionaries and onlookers sang hymns in English and Comanche. After the casket had been lowered into the ground the Indians spread blankets over the coffin, accompanied by the loud grief-stricken cries of the mourners. "All of Quanah's own blankets and the most prized ones of his wives were buried with him to prepare him for his long trip," said a local newspaper report. "There was not a single dry eye among the Comanches," noted Mrs. Becker.[19]

Mrs. Becker told the Mennonite readers of the *Zionsbote* that Quanah Parker "was a good and great leader for his people here on earth, however, he held fast to his old religion." Since his death, she noted, the Indians she worked with were much more willing to use physicians. An unusually high number of deaths occurred in the area in 1911, including several Comanche medicine men; this may also have contributed to increasing willingness to seek medical aid from white doctors.[20] Some medicine men instigated a rumor that Quanah was poisoned by the Cheyennes at Hammon. The failure of their "medicine" to save the chief may have prompted this accusation.[21]

Grave of Cynthia Ann Parker, Post Oak Mission, 1911. Chief Quanah Parker died a few weeks after he had this headstone erected, and was buried next to his mother's tomb.
Credit: Archives & Manuscripts Division of the Oklahoma Historical Society

Four years after Quanah's death, mission workers and the Parker family were shocked to discover his grave desecrated and robbed. Anna Hiebert Gomez on the previous two nights had reported seeing lantern lights in the cemetery. Her colleagues were not concerned and teased her about "seeing ghosts." Reports had been widely circulated at the time of his death that valuables, including a diamond brooch, were buried with the chief. Investigators concluded that the brooch, three rings, and a gold watch chain had been stolen by the robbers. According to Anna Gomez, however, all the thieves got were two silver dollars which had been placed upon Quanah's eyes. His diamond "stick pin," Gomez claimed, was left intact.[22] Mrs. Becker and Parker family members recovered and washed Quanah's scattered bones, and Rev. Becker reburied them, this time in a baby casket.

Funeral of Quanah Parker at Post Oak Mission, February 24, 1911. A.J. Becker, Mennonite Brethren missionary, second from right. David C. Peters, mission worker, is in the second row, far right.
Credit: Archives & Manuscripts Division of the Oklahoma Historical Society

    The six Becker children lived with the presence of death while growing up at Post Oak Mission. Herwanna Becker Barnard later reflected on the "awe-inspiring world of the dead," as she came to know it in her childhood: "Death in its various forms evoked in me an indefinable awe rather than pity or sorrow or fear. Never seeming to touch my own family, but always moving in a special world within my world, death passed through our mission home to the mission church to the mission cemetery, leaving me bewildered and con-

Decoration Day, Post Oak Mission cemetery, circa 1928.
Left: A.J. Becker and son Glenn.   Right: Magdalena Becker and son Peter.

Credit: Courtesy of Glenn Becker

fused."[23]   Observing their parents and the Indian community perform the death rituals did not have a totally negative impact on young Peter and Glenn Becker. As adults both became licensed morticians and established the Becker Funeral Home in Lawton. In a sense, this aspect of the Beckers' ministry, begun during the days of Quanah Parker, continued on until near the end of the century as many Comanches called on the Becker sons to care for their departed loved ones.

Expansion of the Civilization and Christianization Program

On December 15, 1914 Magdalena Becker completed her tenth year as a half-time field matron in the Indian Service. Ernest Stecker, superintendent of the Kiowa Agency, took note of this anniversary by recommending her appointment as a full-time matron at a salary of $600 a year. In a letter to the comissioner of Indian affairs he wrote that Becker was "an unusually loyal and sincere worker," who always kept the welfare of the Indians before her. Not only did she do those things required of her, she willingly tackled "matters pertaining to the home life of our Indians that are often left undone because of their difficulty and unpleasant nature." He emphasized her exceptional interest "in the sick and afflicted," pointing out that for approximately two months she put aside her "personal duties to her family" to care for Indians with typhoid fever. Because of her "loyal, untiring, and efficient" service, Stecker believed she was entitled to the increased pay that a full-time position would provide.[1]

Mrs. Becker initially favored moving to a full-time position, but apparently reconsidered and decided against it. It is difficult to see how she, as a homemaker and church worker, would have had the time or strength to take on more work with the government. The financial costs of raising a large family were a concern, however. The oldest son was nearing college age and the Beckers were committed to sending all their children to college. In her 1914 annual agency report, Mrs. Becker stated she had travelled 1,413 miles by horse team and pointedly noted that, "It is rather hard for the field matrons with a small salary to furnish the team, feed and buggy. Fully half of my salary goes up for this expense." To her surprise, a few months later the government arranged to furnish her a young horse and a new buggy, and to pay the cost of feed.[2] The Mennonite Brethren Conference granted Rev. Becker a $100 raise, bringing his salary to $600 a year. The Beckers also received a special gift of $100 to defray the medical costs encumbered during their siege with typhoid fever.[3] These positive developments helped ease the financial pressures somewhat.

Pleased with the growing success of the mission work, the conference in 1912 accepted the recommendation of missionary Becker to finance the expansion of the Post Oak chapel. A twenty-four by twenty-four square foot addition to the existing structure was authorized. M. M. Just, pastor of the Süd Hoffnungsfeld Mennonite Brethren Church near Fairview, spoke in favor of expansion. He recalled that old Chief Gotebo had predicted the Post Oak "Jesus House" would one day prove to be too small. As usual, Becker not only supervised the building, but did most of the carpentry work himself, although he had some voluntary assistance from Mennonites at Korn and Gotebo.[4]

Anna Hiebert was a great help to the Beckers in the home and church. Like all Mennonite Brethren of her generation, she spoke German and English, but she quickly became fluent in Comanche, Kiowa, and Spanish as well. Born in Russia, Hiebert came to Post Oak from Gotebo, Oklahoma where she had attended a German school. To earn a little extra income she occasionally worked as a housekeeper in Quanah Parker's home, despite the fact that he once told her she was too short and not at all beautiful. After that, it was said she put on her best dress and made herself as presentable as possible whenever the chief came around. The Comanches named her Tia Wy-e-puh, "Little Lady."[5]

On February 16, 1913 Anna married Joe (Jose) Gomez, who worked at the mission as a farmer-rancher and maintenance man. Gomez was a Mexican who crossed the Rio Grande in the early 1900s to work on the railroads. He eventually came to Indiahoma, was converted at the Post Oak Mission, and was employed by the Beckers. Little did Anna and Joe realize as they spoke their vows that they would spend the rest of their days on this mission field. They moved into the house formerly occupied by the Kohfelds and worked side by side with the Beckers.

Their marriage opened the door to an expanded ministry with the Mexicans in the area. Mrs. Gomez helped care for the sick, and over the years transported countless numbers of Indians to the hospital at Lawton, first by team and later by automobile. This valuable ministry to the Comanches also greatly relieved the burden on the Beckers. She interpreted for Comanches and Mexicans who could not speak English. However, it was not until 1936 that Mrs. Gomez was officially commissioned as a Mennonite Brethren missionary to the Indians. Joe Gomez became an official worker under the auspices of the Mennonite Brethren Board of Foreign Missions at about the same time.[6]

A major component of the government's civilization and Christianization program promoted in tandem by Magdalena and A. J. Becker, was the education of Indian youth. Beginning in the 1880s, pressure was exerted on prominent Comanches like Quanah to send their children to Carlisle or other off-reservation boarding schools. There in severely structured programs they were to learn the white ways and then return to their people as examples. On-reservation boarding schools, including one at Fort Sill, were established throughout Indian country by the government and various churches. After allotment and the opening of reservation lands to non-Indians, public district schools became another option for Native Americans.[7] The Mennonite Brethren, perhaps wisely, decided not to establish a school at Post Oak in the early years. They had neither the financial means nor the educational expertise to take it on.

Mrs. Becker originally supported sending Indian children to the boarding schools because they would get regular and more nutritious meals. Perhaps even more important to her was the fact that "there they are made to work."[8] She soon changed her mind and advocated enrolling children in district schools instead. She told the Indian agent that based on her experience families who sent their children to local schools were forced to stay at home more and "do not visit so much." They learned to keep the children neat and clean and to be prompt; they "learn our ways of life much quicker."[9] She also became aware of the heartache and loneliness resulting from the extended absence of children from their families. She was often called upon to write letters for parents and to read to them letters from their children.

On one occasion Mrs. Becker asked the agency when parents could expect their children from Haskell Institute home for the summer. Superintendent C. V. Stinchecum made it very clear to her that such inquiries were not welcome. He stated that personnel in the Indian Office would decide if and when students could return home. Furthermore, he did not believe it necessary for parents to be informed in advance. Becker was directed to instruct families not to bother her or him with any more questions on this issue. In his opinion the students should not be allowed to come home at all in the summer. "It does not seem necessary," he wrote.[10] Although she must have been distressed by this insensitive and arrogant response, Becker did not reveal it in her reply. She dutifully reported to the superintendent that she had announced to her Indians that they were not to ask any more questions about the return of their children.

The Beckers devoted considerable time to Indian youth. For many years Rev. Becker held regularly scheduled religious services at the Fort Sill Indian School. He taught Bible classes in the Indiahoma and Cache high schools. In addition to Sunday school classes, part of each worship service involved the children. Rev. Becker enticed the young pupils to learn Bible verses by promising them a piece of candy if they could recite a verse in front of the congregation. One Sunday a young lad who had forgotten to memorize a verse stood up and recited, "Behold, he who sitteth on a tack shall surely rise again." Even though the youngster could not cite the book of the Bible from which his verse came, the good-humored missionary gave him the candy.

Sunday school was conducted in the afternoon, with the boys and girls segregated into separate classes. Following class time, the pupils engaged in recreational activities. According to Marjorie Kelley, "The boys had chinaberry fights and we girls were busy making mud pies and cakes under the mulberry trees." They also played on a swing set which Rev. Becker made for the children.[11] By 1924 Post Oak Mission had the second largest Sunday School enrollment of twelve missions in the Baptist-Mennonite Brethren Indian Association of Oklahoma.[12] A special Sunday evening service for young people, called Jugendverien in Mennonite circles, was instituted in later years. At the annual Christmas festival the small children and youth presented skits, music, recitations, and other forms of entertainment. Sacks of candy and gifts were then distributed.

Post Oak developed a strong musical tradition. Church gatherings always included singing, of both Comanche and English songs, accompanied by Mrs. Becker on an old pump organ. Several early converts composed Comanche hymns or translated English songs into Comanche. Rev. Becker composed a Comanche hymn that is still popular today. As early as 1907 the tiny congregation had a repertoire of eight Comanche songs. The Beckers wrote: "It is amazing how fast they learn the songs. Even little four-year-old children sing very nice."[13] Dorothy Sunrise Lorentino, honored nationally as an "outstanding Indian Teacher," recalled her childhood at Post Oak: "Mrs. Becker was the best teacher in the world; she was so patient with us mischievous children, and the things she taught us we never forgot."[14]

Mrs. Becker made frequent visits to the schools in the West Cache District. In 1913 there were twenty-eight Indian children attending local schools in her district. The   pupils were generally happy, she reported, well-behaved, and making good progress. Likewise, parents were cooperative, and happy they were allowed to send their children to schools near home. However, in 1917 Dorothy Sunrise, granddaughter of Quanah Parker, was not permitted to enroll in the Cache public school because white patrons said Indian children were dirty, and carried lice and disease. Only after winning a lawsuit against the district were the Sunrise children allowed to attend.

At Becker's sewing classes she instructed mothers how to make clothes for their school children. In one year 109 garments were sewn under her supervision, all patterned after the latest styles in children's clothing. She did not encourage the adult women to forsake the Indian style of dress. The matron agreed that the Indian garments were more comfortable; besides, who could keep up with the changing styles? Comanche mothers did not seem to object, however, to having their young offspring dress like whites.[15]

Group of Post Oak young people enjoying Buffalo Springs Park
Left to right: Winona Sunrise, Herwanna Becker, Addie Wer-yah-vah, Willie Hernasy, Dorothy
Sunrise..
Credit: Archives & Manuscripts Division of the Oklahoma Historical Society

The Indian Office was intent on getting every Comanche child into the classroom. Agents responsible for the disbursement of Indian funds were directed to withhold money from families who did not send their children to school. There were four other regulations that affected the release of Indian monies: (1) the recipient must not be under the influence of alcohol (2) he or she must live a chaste life (3) the family head must work for at least a part of their livelihood, and (4) a couple living together as man and wife must be legally married. According to matron Becker, who frequently aided in the disbursement of funds in her district, the major problems were numbers two and three, not the school attendance requirement.[16]

With the expansion of railway service and the advent of the automobile, A. J. Becker began to itinerate more frequently to Mennonite churches to report on the mission work. He often took Indian Christians along, as early as 1911 taking a delegation of five to the South Hopefield Mennonite Brethren Church at Fairview. The Indians were impressed by the friendly reception they received from the German whites. They also seemed impressed with their smooth-looking skin. One jokingly observed that "the Mennonites must have no worries" since their faces were so wrinkle-free.[17] In 1916 Becker took a group of fifty Comanches to a Singing Convention at Korn. On the return trip, one of the Indians expressed the sentiment of the delegation when he told White Beard, "There are no better people in the world than the Germans." Unlike the "Americans," who thought only about money, "the German Mennonites walk the Jesus Road with both feet; that must be why the Lord blesses them so."[18]

Personal visits, regular reports at church conferences, and frequent letters to the *Zionsbote*, a weekly Mennonite Brethren German newspaper found in virtually every Mennonite Brethren home, all engendered enthusiastic and broad support for the Beckers and Post Oak Mission. All Mennonite Brethren churches had a *Nahverein* (women's sewing circle). These groups provided considerable financial support, as well as material goods, for the sewing organization at Post Oak. The women in the Buhler, Kansas church adopted the name "Herwanna Chapter" for their sewing circle and maintained close ties with the "Magdalena Circle" at Post Oak. The "Herwanna Story" was well-known, and Herwanna became a popular name for girls in Mennonite families for many years.

Over the years a steady stream of visitors found their way through the scenic Wichita Mountains to the grounds of Post Oak. The hospitality of the amiable missionary couple seemed unbounded. No one knows how many meals Mrs. Becker served to church friends, relatives, and acquaintances during their tenure. One Sunday forty members of the Bessie, Oklahoma Mennonite Brethren Church arrived for a brief visit. Fortunately they brought along food for themselves and their hosts. Although this was a planned visit, surprise calls were not uncommon. The Becker children learned that a certain sign from their mother meant they were to cut back on their food intake in order to leave enough for the guests. Entertaining visitors un-

The Becker's home at Post Oak Mission where they raised six children and welcomed countless numbers of Indian, white and Mexican visitors.   Credit: Courtesy of Glenn Becker

doubtedly helped promote support for the Indian mission work, but it also increased the work load of a staff already overburdened.[19]

Becker and "his Indians" also frequently traveled to other mission stations, primarily Baptist, to participate in religious services. Post Oak Mission was accepted as a regular and official participant in the annual meetings of the Indian Baptist Association of Oklahoma. In July 1915 Becker accompanied more than thirty of his members to Anadarko where representatives of eleven different tribes were convened for an associational meeting. Typically, evangelism, or "soul winning," Bible training, and fellowship were the major thrusts of these protracted gatherings. Baptist denominational leaders also discussed administrative and other business matters with their missionaries. With a dozen different languages represented, communication was cumbersome at best. Whenever an Indian spoke to the assembly, his words were translated into English; then interpreters translated them into the other native languages represented in the audience. Even Becker admitted that this drawn-out procedure could get boring. Since both the Baptists and the Mennonite Brethren practiced immersion, these joint meetings were always concluded with a baptismal service, with the missionaries baptizing any converts from their own field. At Anadarko, Becker baptized two such candidates and received them into the membership of Post Oak Mission.[20]   The close relationship that developed between Post Oak Mission and the Baptist missions tended to blur Mennonite Brethren distinctives. The

Baptists' preaching emphasis on "soul winning" reinforced Becker's own approach. Undoubtedly reflecting Baptist influence, he soon organized a Soul Saving Club at Post Oak. There was little emphasis at the associational meetings on the nurture of new Indian Christians. Even the Bible training sessions were primarily geared to teach Indian converts how to become "soul winners." At Post Oak Mission the "soul winning" emphasis also appears to have been much stronger than the "soul nurturing" aspect. The extensive service outreach into the broader Indian community by the Beckers remained a distinguishing characteristic of the Mennonite Brethren mission, however.

The Beckers had relatively little contact with missionaries from denominations other than Baptist, although the agency's missionaries occasionally met to discuss common concerns and Magdalena had good relations with other missionary wives who worked as field matrons. The practice of infant baptism by the Methodist, Presbyterian, and Dutch Reformed missions was contrary to Mennonite theology. When a member of the Dutch Reformed Mission sought membership in the Post Oak church, he had to be rebaptized first, in true Anabaptist tradition. On the other hand, the transfer of memberships between Deyo and Post Oak missions was readily approved.

The annual associational meetings were held at the different mission stations on a rotating basis, with Post Oak hosting them about once every ten years. The first time was in 1922. There were generally about twelve missions from western Oklahoma represented, including a few from the Cheyenne-Arapaho Agency.

In keeping with Becker's mission strategy, Post Oak sponsored at least one extended *Zeltversammlung* (tent meeting) each year, often bringing in guest evangelists. Rev. M. M. Just of Fairview was a frequent speaker in the years before 1920. The Indians dubbed the large, stocky, popular preacher, "Rev. Big Chief." C. N. Hiebert, N. N. Hiebert, J. J. Wiebe, and H. W. Lohrenz were Mennonite Brethren ministers often called upon to conduct meetings in subsequent years. During the first two decades of this century it was difficult to find Mennonite Brethren clergy who could preach effectively in English since church services were still conducted in the German language. At times Becker had to rely on the Baptists to provide him a guest revivalist; E. C. Deyo was often utilized. Becker frequently preached at similar gatherings at neighboring missions.

Indian baptismal scene. Post Oak Mission and the Amercian Baptist's Deyo Mission frequently held joint Indian Camp meetings which generally concluded with a baptismal service. Standing in the water on the right is missionary E. C. Deyo. Credit: The Center for Mennonite Brethren Studies, Fresno CA

A typical Post Oak camp meeting of the early years might be the four-day event held in September 1915. In preparation for the large turnout expected, the members purchased and butchered four head of beef, and hauled in ten wagonloads of wood for camp fires. The encampment consisted of forty-three lodges, with two or more families in each. A large number of Kiowas from Saddle Mountain also attended. Their main contribution, according to Becker, was "their loud singing." Each morning before sunup an elderly Indian, Ni-yah, went through the lodge area giving a loud wake-up call for the sunrise prayer service. Some mornings his loud shouting continued well past sunrise; he would not cease until he had aroused everyone from their slumber. Mid-morning a general assembly was held. A youth service, led by a young Kiowa who was "strong in the faith and in English," took place each afternoon. In the evening a two-to-three hour singing and preaching service was conducted by a missionary from Watonga, Oklahoma. He was a replacement for Rev. Just who could not come that year. The Kiowas sat on one side of the tent and the Comanches on the other, with an interpreter positioned in front of each group. In between services—and perhaps during—there

Early-day camp meeting at Post Oak Mission church with the Wichita Mountains in the background.
Credit: The Center for Mennonite Brethren Studies, Fresno CA

Indian encampment at Post Oak Mission, circa 1920. Preaching the gospel of salvation at camp meetings lasting a week or longer was a common mission strategy in southwestern Oklahoma.
Credit: Courtesy of Elsie Becker

was considerable eating, recreation, and visiting. On Sunday many whites attended the concluding worship service and baptism at the Post Oak dam.

Becker frequently expressed disappointment at the few converts garnered at the tent meetings. Yet he continued to follow this mission approach. The communal camp gatherings were always well-attended and enjoyed by the Indians. And, as Becker explained, protracted exposure to the gospel was helpful since "with the saving of Indians, it goes very slow." Not all the "convicted sinners" who responded to the altar call were baptized immediately. Becker said he was careful not to "baptize anyone until we're sure they're really born again." His follow-up meetings in homes often proved productive in gaining converts.[21]

In 1917 the mission dining hall was expanded with a twelve by twenty-eight foot addition. The additional space made it possible for Indian families to store their dishes for Sunday use at the mission. A two-room building for a clinic and the sewing circle meetings was also constructed. Fourteen volunteers from Korn did most of the construction work, under the supervision of contractor Dan Schmidt. That same year, Maria Heinrichs of Kirk, Colorado was assigned by the Mennonite Brethren Conference, at a salary of $250 annually, to assist Mrs. Becker. Both these steps were taken to meet pressing needs in space and personnel needs at the mission. Rev. Becker was exuberant: "So many good things have come our way. When the need is the greatest, then God's help is the nearest."[22] Heinrichs' responsibilities were to help with the housework, sewing sessions, house visits, and funerals.

The year 1917 also marked the tenth anniversary of Becker taking on the duties as head missionary. In the decade since 1907 he had baptized ninety-nine people and brought them into church membership. Twenty-four had died or moved away, leaving an active roll of sixty-six. Although he could rejoice at the "ninety and nine" that had been brought safely into the fold, he expressed concern about the hundredth "lost sheep" not yet found. Reflecting on his service, Becker observed: "God has given much peace and joy in the work, and with His help we have had success in gaining true Indian Christians." Comanche members were assuming more responsibility–a process the Beckers promoted. Included in the corps of strong indigenous leaders were George Koweno, the first deacon, his wife Wi-e-puh (Mary), Shelby Tenequer, and Reuben Te-hau-no. They were capable of leading services and were eager to evangelize others. When

Herman Asenap suffered an extended bout with typhoid fever in 1916, the latter two served as interpreters. Her-na-sy was identified as "one of our best workers," and No Hand, the first baptized convert, was always available to provide assistance and enliven the proceedings.[23]

Becker was also pleased that financial support by the congregation was growing; the total giving for all causes in 1916 was $352. "They have done right well," Becker observed. There were some distressing problems: gambling, fornication, and peyote use. But despite their "many tears," and hard work—conducting as many as 150 services a year, for example—there was no longer any talk of resigning. Becker informed the constituency: "I love the Indians; I love the brothers and sisters of the MB Church who uphold them; and, most of all, I love God." It appeared that White Beard was convinced that God had called him to live among the Comanches, and lead them on the straight and narrow "Jesus Way" to eternal life. All indications are that Magdalena Becker felt the same way.[24]

In recognition and appreciation for his many years of missionary work, the conference raised Becker's salary to $800 a year. Subsequently it would be set at $1000 annually, bringing it in line with the salaries of Mennonite Brethren missionaries to India, which ranged from $1000 to 1200 a year.[25]

In 1918 Herwanna, at age ten, became the fourth Becker child to be baptized. Some Comanches, probably in jest, asked eight-year-old Sammie Becker why he did not also take the "Jesus Road." "Tit-tet" (Too little), he replied. The father was proud of his son's answer, not only because it was correct Mennonite theology, but also because he could respond in the tribal tongue. All the Becker children learned to understand and speak Comanche. William, whose Indian name was "Big Eagle," would later write a master's thesis on the structure of the Comanche language.

On the Sunday of Herwanna's baptism, No Hand arrived at church feeling ill. But he reported that while observing White Beard immersing his young daughter, "My heart was glad, and my body got well."[26] The Comanche woman, Her-wa-nee, after whom the Beckers had named their daughter, continued to be an inspiration in church and community. In November 1918 the Indian Service placed her name on the honor roll of exemplary housekeepers.[27]

Field Matron Activities

Magdalena Becker's work load continued unabated. She usually spent three days a week on the road and one day at the mission working with Indian women and their families. Many times she worked more than the four days per week required for half-time field matrons. A strong, sturdy woman, she rarely missed work on account of sickness. When pregnant with her son Glenn, she worked until the day of his birth, February 26, 1918, but then took leave for about a month. A review of the records from 1916-22 shows that Mrs. Becker consistently had more Indian contacts than the other field matrons of the Kiowa and Comanche agency. The twelve-month period from November 1915 to November 1916, was a fairly typical year for her. During that time she made 480 family visits with 1,600 Indians reached, ministered to 135 sick persons, composed 550 letters for Indians or corresponded on their behalf, directed 26 sewing sessions, registered 11 deaths and helped with their burial; and registered 15 births, naming many of the newborn.[1]

An increasing amount of Mrs. Becker's time was devoted to marital counseling and settling family disputes, an activity not noted in her reports prior to about 1915. On several occasions she was called to intervene in wife battering cases. Whether or not wife beating was one of white civilization's "gifts" to Indians, as some Comanches claimed, domestic violence in Becker's jurisdiction had increased. She attributed this in part to multiple-family homes and recommended that the superintendent issue a directive prohibiting it. During a three-day dance at Che-bah-tah's home in August 1919, "Mother" Becker was called to six homes to settle violent quarrels. "Wiping [sic] wifes [sic] was the fruit" of the extended dance festivities, she complained.[2]

Caring for the sick continued to be one of Mrs. Becker's most important and appreciated contributions to the welfare of Indian people. Even though they could get free medical services at the Indian hospital near Lawton, many Comanches feared to go there. Instead, they chose to come to Post Oak Mission. As in the earlier years some continued to camp on the grounds for an extended period. Indians who otherwise showed no interest in the mission would bring their sick to the Beckers' home. "It gives us much work but we do it gladly," Magdalena told *Zionsbote* readers. But she was hurt that a patient had recently stolen some of their personal belongings while at the station.[3]

The more serious cases would be transported to the hospital by the Beckers or Anna Gomez.

The most frequent illnesses reported between 1916 and 1924 were measles, pneumonia, consumption, whooping cough, typhoid fever, tuberculosis, diarrhea, and influenza. There were deaths attributed to each of those maladies. Three epidemics swept through Becker's district in 1918. Measles struck early in the year, a siege of whooping cough in late summer, and the worldwide influenza epidemic in December. During the first two weeks, Becker reported thirty cases of influenza and one death due to the disease. The following week she herself was in bed with the illness, but she missed only two days of work.

According to Becker's reports for 1918, there were six deaths where the deceased had been treated only by Indian medicine men, or "mescal men," as she also called them. She believed those deaths could have been prevented with "proper" medical care.[4] Often non-Christian religious rituals were included in native healing practices contributing to the Beckers' resistence to medicine men. Although the medicine men's treatment was crude and ineffective at times, as was also the case with some pioneer white doctors, the use of herbs apparently helped in certain cases, and the patient's confidence in a tribal medicine man may have at times induced beneficial results.[5]

The continuing influence of medicine men was one sign that the government's acculturation program was lagging. There were others. Early in 1919 Mrs. Becker learned that Baldwin Parker, Quanah Parker's son, was living with two wives. Apparently he thought that since his father had been able to ignore the white man's marriage laws, he could do the same. Not in Mrs. Becker's district! She sent one of the wives, Jennie Too-ah-voomi, packing. "We will have to handle this case right soon," she warned the Indian superintendent, "as others will follow their example."[6] In fact, some believed Baldwin Parker was incapable of providing proper care for even one wife and family. In June 1919 his wife Nora was forced to farm out their children while she was hospitalized. She sent a letter requesting the Indian agency to release her funds so she could help provide for their upkeep. She also hoped to repair the house, buy some furniture, and get a "team and hack." "Mrs. Becker knows I can keep my house clean," she wrote. Louise Driscoll, a field matron who was keeping the Parkers' youngest child, recommended Nora be given a monthly allowance, "but with strings on it." Driscoll had been informed that Nora gave her money to her "worthless husband" and feared the children, "destitute of clothing," would not benefit from the funds unless someone intervened. Driscoll was distressed to learn that Nora's funds were already depleted. The agency superintendent advised that they had recently drawn the entire balance to the credit of Baldwin Parker for the benefit of her children. Indications are the superintendent and Mrs. Becker did not share Driscoll's hostility toward Nora's husband.[7]

Peyote use, ceremonial dances, and Indian powwows increased in the years after Quanah Parker's death. Mennonite Brethren found smoking and dancing, for whatever purpose, abominable. But beyond moral or religious implications, Mrs. Becker, in her role as field matron, saw the prevalence of dance activities as a deterrent to work. Dances took her Comanches away from their homes, gardens, and fields, and rendered impossible a "normal home life." Travelling from one location to another, setting up camp, and dancing was not, of course, unusual in Comanche culture. Indeed, Comanche Christians frequently took their families to protracted religious camp meetings where tepees were erected, food prepared, and singing, praying, and preaching went on late into the night. Quanah Parker once showed up at the Deyo Mission during a three-day religious encampment and told the participants they should go home and work, like the government desired. A mission worker expressed resentment of the Comanche, calling him a "fake chief" who was "too proud to go the Jesus Road."[8]

In July 1920 Che-bah-tah hosted a week-long dance at his home, with a large crowd in attendance. Mrs. Becker visited the event and declared it "time and money wasted." Those Indians "could make $5 and $6 a day" if they would only work. Later in the month she found many of her absentee West Cache Indians camped with a group of 300 Kiowas and Comanches near the Forest Headquarters, "dancing and having pictures taken to be used in the movies." Movies were also on the Mennonite "sin" list. Magdalena used her influence to have the dances stopped and the camp broken up. "The dances and large gatherings week after week are ruining our Indian boys and girls," she reported. They had been going on for about three months at different places with "no work done during these days." She pled for assistance "to have this thing checked as they will be paupers before long and the hospitals will be filled with boys and girls infected by different decease [sic]."[9]

Magdalena Becker's aggressiveness made her some enemies. In a public meeting with the commissioner of Indian affairs in February 1920, Post Oak Jim accused her and her husband of making false charges against him that resulted in the withholding of his money. The full story was that the Beckers reported his gambling operations, netting him a jail sentence in December 1919.[10] Mrs. Becker maintained a list of gamblers for the authorities, but charged that the county lacked "a set of faithful officers to enforce the law." Gamblers kept an eagle eye out for the feisty field matron. "Sometimes when I am a half a mile from the gambling place they scatter in all directions," she told superintendent J. A. Buntin, who shared her concern about gambling.[11]

Becker also dutifully reported any illegal peyote meetings encountered on her field trips. Oklahoma's official recognition of the Native American Church in 1918, with the legal right to use peyote in its religious ceremonies, was a setback to the Christianization element of the civilization program. Peyote adherents fostered not only the revival of old religious customs, but other tribal traditions as well. Post Oak Mission was in the heart of the area most active in the development and spread of the peyote movement. Although the impact on attendance at that mission was negligible, missionaries in southwestern Oklahoma found stiff competition from the Native American Church.[12]

World War I had slight impact on the work of Post Oak Mission. Magdalena Becker was appointed to the Executive Committee for Red Cross Work in Comanche County, and a Red Cross Auxiliary was established at the mission. Indian women sewed hospital garments, medical wraps, and clothing for war refugees. Seven men associated with Post Oak Mission, including Daniel Becker, were drafted but all returned home safely. Field matrons were instructed to push the Indians into buying Liberty Bonds; names of purchasers and amounts were to be sent to the agency office. Some Indians responded, but in 1919 Becker was asked to explain why her charges were not buying government thrift stamps. She notified the Anadarko office that she was not going to press the issue on people who had no money. Due to a total crop failure her Comanches had to struggle just to get through the winter, "with sickness, Dr. bills, etc," she stated.[13]

Mrs. Becker was also aggressive in the pursuit of justice for aggrieved Indians. When an Indian woman gave birth to an illegitimate child fathered by a white man, she took steps to have him pay some of the bills. When he refused to take responsibility, the agency office asked the county attorney, L. M. Gensman, to file charges. Gensman warned that the Oklahoma paternity law, which he referred to as the "bastardy" law, was "pretty much a farce." One could serve papers on the accused, but that was usually the end of it. Nevertheless, he wrote, "anything you want done will certainly be done. I might add, we will do anything you want done right or wrong, but I wouldn't want to put that down on paper." With that open-ended assurance, the Indian superintendent asked Becker to take the woman to Lawton to see Gensman. She had already done so on her own. On October 6 1919, Becker reported that papers had been served on the defendant and that a court case had been docketed. In early February 1920 she testified as a witness in the case. The result is revealed in a notation by Superintendent Stinchecum on a letter from Becker to the agency: "Judgement for $300 received." What the county attorney had done, and whether it was right or wrong, was not revealed, but it appears that Mrs. Becker helped secure at least a measure of justice for this young Comanche woman.[14]

Post Oak Mission April 1927
Credit: Cornelius Wall photo. Center for Mennonite Brethren Studies, Hillsboro, KS

Hard Times and Good Times:
The 20s and 30s

The collapse of farm prices in the decade of the 1920s and the nearly total breakdown of the American economy during the Great Depression had serious implications for the work of Post Oak Mission and the welfare of the Comanches. In 1921 the budget for Post Oak from General Conference funds was $2,032. In addition, the mission received $565 in special gifts. In 1922 the budget was essentially the same but special gifts from the constituency had dropped to $269. Because of decreased giving the budget was reduced to $1,500 in 1923, and special gifts dropped to only $150. Rev. Becker reported that because of the shortfall in special gifts they had been able to distribute only $15.05 to the poor and could buy very little candy to bag for their Christmas program. They had also cancelled a camp meeting.[1]

Ten years later the financial situation of the Mennonite Brethren and Post Oak had worsened. The General Conference budget for the mission in 1933 was only $1,000, and Becker was warned it would probably be cut another $200 the following year. The missionary's salary was reduced to $700 a year, with only a $50 car allowance. Becker traveled between 13,000 and 15,000 miles a year, in his own car, at a cost of approximately $400.[2]

An economic situation that was extremely serious for the Mennonite people was nothing short of catastrophic for the Comanches. American Indians were the poorest of the poor during the depression years. After allotment the average per capita holding of land on the Kiowa-Comanche Reservation was about 160 acres; by 1934 it had dropped to 17 acres. Land sales to provide the necessities of life, home improvements, or medical care, as well as fee patents forced on the Indians, drastically diminished Comanche landholdings. Government policy assisted the Indians in disposing of their land. Agents implemented a Department of the Interior recommendation that all "surplus" Indian lands ought to be leased or sold "for the benefit and in the interest of all the people in the country" instead of being kept for the individual Indian. Agents also assisted local white citizens to obtain valuable concessions from allottees. Allegations that leasing improprieties occurred at the Kiowa Agency persist to this day.[3] Loss of land, lack of rental and lease income, and few marketable skills left the Comanches deeply impoverished. Even those who kept their land could hardly eke out a living during the drought-ridden thirties, as many Mennonite farmers living on much more productive acres could attest. "Never have I had so many come to my home and ask for bread," Mrs. Becker wrote in 1930. "We have divided up sometimes till it hurts."[4]

The avarice and unethical practices of area merchants contributed to the plight of the poor Comanches. Lacking experience or knowledge in financial and business affairs, many fell victim to price gouging, excessive interest rates, and sales pressure. Recognizing this, Mrs. Becker frequently accompanied Indians to business establishments to make sure they got the "right prices," and were not coaxed into buying unnecessary or expensive items. "The Indian by nature always wants the best," she stated, and thus were vulnerable to the sales pitches of shopkeepers. Unprincipled merchants always seemed to know how much money each family received in payments and set their prices accordingly. Prior to the arrival of the Beckers, one banker was found guilty of charging Indians interest rates of 150 to 3,360 percent.[5] Throughout the 1920s and early 1930s, Mrs. Becker continued to supervise the purchase of such goods as clothing for school children, buggies, furniture, and other items.

Proponents of the allotment policy had predicted that individual ownership of land would provide the Indian with incentive to become a thriving self-sufficent yeoman farmer, anxious to move into the mainstream of American life. Three decades after allotment had been forced upon the Comanches, it was clear that this goal had not been achieved. Non-Indians benefited the most from the policy. Not only had whites obtained the "surplus" lands of the Indians, they were rapidly acquiring their allotments as well. By 1934 most Indians had only a small plot of ground left to live on. The little income they had came from agricultural, oil, or grass leases which were handled for them by the Indian Office. Adding to the problem, in 1932 over half the payments for land rentals were delinquent.[6] To withdraw money from their accounts, Indians had to submit a formal request to the area superintendent and await his approval. Agency approval was required to build a house, receive major medical care, buy a team, buggy, farm implements, tools, or feed, or fill any immediate needs. Most requests were submitted by the field matrons in the form of special reports. Mrs. Becker wrote thousands of such requests for the Comanches. In 1922 her special reports numbered five to sixteen per week; in subsequent years they rarely fell below fourteen and at times went as high as forty-two and fifty-seven per week.

One Indian official, in defense of the close supervision of Indian funds, stated: "If you gave them all their money, within six months it would all be gone and the counties would have to take care of them." He warned the Indians that their payments would eventually end, and then they "must work or starve." Unfortunately, as the sources of their income were drying up in the 20s and 30s, there was little or no work in southwestern Oklahoma for Indians or non- Indians.[7]

Not all Indians disposed of their land, or lost it through devious means. Ur-he-yah, who joined the Post Oak Mission Church in 1926 at age seventy, had extensive holdings of allotted and inherited lands. It was said that he had a substantial income and regularly gave the tithe to the church.[8] Because of his "considerable money," the agency physician approved sending Ur-he-yah's wife to the Mayo Clinic for specialized medical care.[9]

Missionary Becker did not promise the Indians that acceptance of the white man's religion would bring them economic prosperity. He knew that Mennonite history documented a different story. One Comanche woman was able to testify to that also. Before her conversion to Christianity, she said, she was a gambler, and "was always rich." Then she became a Christian and gave up gambling. "Now," she said, "I am always poor." But she was willing to pay that price to follow the road that missionary Becker said would lead to eternal life.[10]

Despite financial difficulties, the work at Post Oak continued to expand. The following list demonstrates the diversity and scope of missionary activities: all-day services and a noon meal each Sunday at the mission; chapel services every third Sunday at Fort Sill Indian School; monthly ministry to staff and patients at the Indian Hospital; bi-monthly or monthly meetings of the Ladies Missionary Circle, 4-H Club, Farm Women's Club, Canning Club; weekly prayer meetings; Bible classes in the Indiahoma and Cache high schools; quarterly and annual meetings with the Indian Baptist Association; annual camp meeting at Post Oak; several Bible conferences a year; funerals; weddings; home visitation; and special programs and meals at Christmas (two days), Easter, Decoration Day, and Thanksgiving.

In 1928, after more than a quarter of a century on the mission field, the seemingly indefatigable missionary couple finally confessed that "the work is too much for us. We can't keep up with it all."[11]

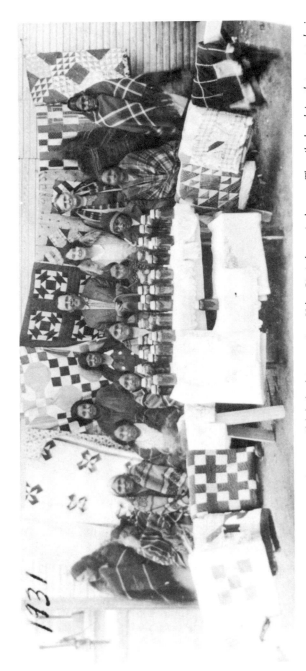

The Magdalena Sewing Circle and the Post Oak Canning Club display their wares. Agent Hobart Rice is the man in the center. The quilts show designs that were popular in the 1920s and 1930s.
Credit: Archives & Manuscripts Division of the Oklahoma Historical Society

They asked the mission board for assistance for Mrs. Becker and a person to take care of the buildings and grounds. Unfortunately, instead of providing more personnel, the Foreign Mission Board was soon forced to initiate cuts in their budget.[12]

Indian leadership took some of the load off the Beckers' shoulders. The church's first deacon, George Koweno, had been ordained in 1911. In 1930 two additional men, Ur-he-yah and Felix Koweno (also spelled Kowena), were selected to assume the responsibilities of that office. Ur-he-yah was a respected elder in the tribe and Felix, an ex-professional baseball player, was the young stepson of George Koweno. Deacon George Koweno's death in 1936 was a serious loss to the Beckers and the congregation. A strong traditionalist until his conversion, he took up farming, discarded his long hair, and gave up dancing. He had built a little house at the mission station where his family lived on weekends while they attended services. In 1933 he served as a chief informant for E. Adamson Hoebel, anthropologist with the Santa Fe Laboratory of Anthropology, in his study of Comanche culture. Koweno's contributions to that study are incorporated in the findings published by Hoebel and Ernest Wallace.[13] Koweno's life was portrayed by the missionaries as an example of a benighted "heathen" transformed into a civilized and outstanding Christian citizen.[14]

Comanche leaders in the Post Oak Mission church.
Left to right: Herman Asenap, interpreter; Jim Che-bah-tah, interpreter and deacon; Pahcheka,
interpreter; Felix Koweno, deacon and interpreter; A. J. and Magdalena Becker, April 17, 1938.
Credit: Courtesy of Glenn Becker

Dedication of Quanah Parker monument, May 4, 1930. Rev. Becker was a featured speaker.
Seated left to right: Lewis Ware, Jim Nance, Baldwin Parker, Lt. Col. Leslie McNair, Harry Stroud.
Standing on right: Rev. and Mrs. Becker, Herman Asenap, and To-pay.
Credit: Coutesy of Glenn Becker

The deacons were now allowed to assume more authority than in the past, church committees and a council were elected, and leaders were selected to direct the youth program. Becker's sermons continued to be interpreted into the Comanche and Spanish languages, but youth services were now conducted only in English. For many years the mission board budgeted $50 annually as stipends for the interpreters. James Che-bah-tah, whose father's dancing activities had provoked Mrs. Becker's ire, became a Christian in 1936 and joined the team of interpreters. Later he would also become a deacon.

On May 4, 1930 Post Oak Mission received considerable statewide and national attention. On that day a monument to Quanah Parker was unveiled and dedicated at the Post Oak Mission Cemetery. The crowd in attendance was variously estimated between 3,500 and 5,000 people. The monument, authorized by an act of Congress in 1926, was a seventeen-foot-tall red, granite spire quarried in the Wichita Mountains. The Mennonite Brethren Church donated the portion of ground on which Quanah and Cynthia Ann Parker were buried. This ceremony was a formal recognition by the government of Quanah's signal role in leading his people from a nomadic life to accomodation with the dominant white society. Through his force and intelligence, and his romantic origins, the great warrior-chief had achieved enduring renown. John Nance, Speaker of the Oklahoma House of Representatives, gave an address extolling the virtues of this talented Indian. J. A. Buntin, representing the Bureau of Indian Affairs, spoke of Parker's support of education and his twenty trips to Washington on behalf of Indian interests. An old companion, Quassah-Yah, gave a tribute in Comanche.

Rev. Becker was the featured speaker. The longtime missionary it was noted, had probably known the chief better than any other white man.[15] Becker told of Parker's religious tendencies saying that although he never joined the church, he had on various occasions urged his people "to heed the words of Missionary Becker." Baldwin Parker spoke a few words of appreciation on behalf of the Parker family. The monument was unveiled by Quassah-Yah and two of Quanah Parker's granddaughters, Rowena Asenap and Alberta Clark. An honor guard from Fort Sill fired a salute over the grave. Without doubt, Quanah would have relished the praises showered upon him that day. His imposing monument, standing next to the prominent tombstone of Cynthia Ann Parker, attracted many visitors to Post Oak over the years.[16]

To-nar-cy, left and To-pay, right, last two wives of Quanah Parker, standing with Lena Banks, field matron at the dedication of the Parker monument. To-pay was a member of the Mennonite Brethren Mission church for twenty years.
Credit: Archives & Manuscript Divison of the Oklahoma Historical Society

The Loss of "Mother" Becker

Declining health began to take its toll on both Magdalena and A. J. Becker. Her troublesome medical problems were undiagnosed; he suffered from a heart condition. On June 30, 1932, after twenty-eight years as a half time field matron (though she never tackled anything "half-time") Mrs. Becker resigned from her position.

Magdalena Becker holds the distinction of having served longer than any other field matron of the Kiowa Indian Agency, and possibly longer than any other matron in the program's forty-eight-year history. Commissioner of Indian Affairs Charles Burke created the Bureau of Public Health Nursing in the Medical Division of the Indian Service in 1924 and field nurses gradually replaced field matrons as they resigned or retired. On the Kiowa Agency, nurses began to replace the matrons in 1928. In 1934, two years after Mrs. Becker retired, there were only six matrons remaining in the Indian Service. By 1938 the program had been phased out completely. A new emphasis on preserving rather than destroying Indian cultures, and on the need for trained social and health workers, meant the field matron program was no longer considered viable. Also, there were complaints about the quality of the personnel filling field matron positions on many reservations.[1]

Critics of the field matron program charged that the matrons had accomplished little, if anything, in "civilizing" Indian women and their families and assimilating them into American society. Magdalena Becker, however, could attest to some positive changes during her tenure. Undeniably she had made a significant impact on the lives of Comanche women and their families in the West Cache District. From her they learned the skills of good housekeeping, financial management, child care, sanitation, preventive health practices, cooking, sewing, quilting, gardening, and canning. Many Comanches incorporated her instructions into their daily lives. Becker was more effective than many matrons because she worked side by side with the Indians. Her teaching style was personal "hands-on."

Another key to Magdalena's success was her fluency in the Comanche language. Many field matrons required interpreters, who were hard to secure because of lack of funds. Her obvious concern for Indian welfare, and her sacrificial spirit, won their confidence, respect, and love. She consistently practiced those Christian virtues her husband proclaimed from the pulpit on Sundays. This drew Indians to her, and to Post Oak Mission. She held a holistic view of Christian ministry; her field matron duties were not seen as separate from her service as a missionary.

One of the changes she witnessed as matron was in Indian housing. In the early years over half the families she visited lived in tents or tepees. Even as late as the 1920s a good number, whether by choice or necessity, were still in tents. As a result of the concerted efforts of superintendent J. A. Buntin, virtually all the Indians lived in houses by the end of the 1920's. The Indian Office lauded the success of the house-building campaign as another example of progress in acculturation. However, the Indians were induced to sell their surplus lands to pay for their homes, thus depriving them of income from agricultural rentals, and in some cases, oil leases. Many Comanches, after paying construction costs, found themselves without money. They were forced to pawn or sell machinery, stock, furniture, and other goods to buy groceries. In the end they had a house, but less land, less personal property, and limited means to pay for upkeep and repair.[2]

An area of progress of particular importance to Mrs. Becker was the relative improvement in health conditions. When the Beckers first came to the reservation they were told the Indians were a vanishing race—they would soon die off. For a few years it appeared to them that this might be true. But an aggressive educational program, the opening of an Indian hospital, and the personal care of people like Magdelena Becker helped turn the tide. The Indian population in the area increased forty-three percent during her twenty-eight years as a field matron, indicating how significantly conditions had improved. Since the Kiowa Agency hospital had only one physician and a forty-two bed capacity, it would appear that the matrons, although generally untrained in medical care, deserve much more credit for improved health statistics than they have received. Becker was in the forefront of those promoting the children's immunization program against smallpox, typhoid fever, and diphtheria in her district. A persistent critic of medicine men, she was pleased to see their influence greatly diminished by the 1930s, viewing this as another sign of progress. Shortly before her retirement, the veteran field matron recommended to the commissioner of Indian affairs that the medical services of the Kiowa Agency be expanded by opening a branch hospital or clinic in the West Cache area. She believed that free medical care needed to be more accessible; many Comanches could not afford autos or the services of private doctors in Cache or Indiahoma.[3]

Perhaps the biggest disappointment for Becker was the fact that the Indians were still far from self-sufficient, and mired in a state of dependency. Of the more than four thousand Kiowas and Comanches on the agency in 1929, only 415 were engaged in farming and only 136 were engaged in other businesses. (By counting every Indian who planted a garden as a farmer, the Bureau of Indian Affairs misleadingly claimed that seventy-five percent were engaged in "some sort of agriculture"). Poor policies, government mismanagement, and the severe economic depression had brought the Indians to a low state. They appeared ready for a "New Deal."[4]

During the early period of her employment, Mrs. Becker generally reached 600 to 900 Indians per year in fulfilling her duties. In 1923-24, the last year for which official records are available, she personally reached an average of about 500 Comanches each month.[5] From the beginning of her career until the very end, she traveled by buggy. In twenty-eight years she bounced many thousands of miles across the rugged Comanche reserve, enjoying the pleasant and enduring the foul weather conditions that marked Oklahoma's changeable climate. Throughout, she retained a positive attitude toward "her Comanches," about whom she frequently said, "They are willing to learn and improve themselves." Agency personnel and other observers could only marvel at her spiritual motivation, physical stamina, and indomitable spirit. To the Comanches she was a teacher, nurse, mentor, counselor, peacemaker, friend—small wonder they called her "Mother Becker." At the close of her last day as field matron Magdalena wrote in her Monthly Time Book, "Good-by hard work as field matron . . . will be easier now with just mission work."[6]

In 1930, despite their own admission of being overextended, the Beckers began a Mexican outreach program at Richards Spur, a rock crushing work camp thirty-five miles northeast of Post Oak. For several years Mexicans in the Post Oak area had been transported in an open truck to the mission for services. Becker's sermons were interpreted into Spanish by Anna Gomez. Some thirty to thirty-five Mexicans regularly attended Sunday services, joining the approximately 100 Indians who worshipped there. Some Mennonites questioned the wisdom of expanding the work to Richards Spur in view of the added cost in time and money. Becker believed expansion of the Mexican ministry to outlying communities was right and proper. After all, they are our neighbors, he said, "and no one else is concerned about them." After her retirement as matron Mrs. Becker was also more free to devote time to a work in which she was greatly interested. Thirty-five Mexican converts had been baptized by 1935, many coming from the Richards Spur substation.

Mexican workers constructing a concrete building to support a twelve hundred gallon water tank at Post Oak. Reinforced with thirty-four old Ford frames, Rev Becker "guaranteed" it for a thousand years.
Credit: Archives & Manuscript Divison of the Oklahoma Historical Society.

In spring 1936 the Beckers and a Mexican ministry team began to hold meetings in Lawton. Rapid success in gaining converts at Post Oak, Richards Spur, and Lawton inspired the Beckers to recommend to the mission board that a separate mission church be established for the Mexicans on the outskirts of Lawton. Failing that, a church should be built for them on the Post Oak grounds. By the end of 1936, the total number of Mexicans baptized by Becker had reached eighty. So many of these new converts were attending services at Post Oak that the Indians were "beginning to feel crowded out," according to Becker.[7]

In fall 1936 the Mennonite Brethren General Conference accepted the Beckers' recommendation and authorized the establishment of a mission at Lawton. Construction of a chapel would begin as soon as the constituency contributed enough funds specifically designated for the project. The city of Lawton, following a plea from Mrs. Becker, agreed to donate a site. With the receipt of many small sacrificial gifts, and donated labor from Corn, all prompted by the promotional skills of Rev. Becker, a structure was erected. It stood twenty-six by forty-eight feet and included two rooms for a resident missionary.

Dedication of the Mennonite Brethren Mexican Mission. Lawton, June 6, 1937.
Credit: Courtesy of Glenn Becker

The "Post Oak Mexican Mission" was dedicated on June 6, 1937. At the time it was the only mission established for Mexicans—Protestant or Catholic—between Oklahoma City and Wichita Falls, Texas.[8] Supervision of the new mission's work was assigned to Rev. Becker. Among the pioneer missionaries and workers at Lawton were Rev. Joe Gonzales, an American Baptist missionary who had joined the Post Oak Mission church in 1936; Salvador Rivera, a young convert whom the Beckers had virtually adopted; Anna Gomez; J. J. Reimer; Ike Gonzales; and Ben Luna. All were fluent in Spanish, undoubtedly a significant factor in the mission's early evangelistic success.

The challenge and excitement of launching the Mexican project rejuvenated the Beckers. Rev. Becker not only solicited the funds, he also drew the plans and worked with hammer and saw to bring the church to completion. But the effort took its toll. In November 1937 his heart problem flared up again, and the doctor ordered him to severely limit his activities. He had already taken steps to reduce his weight and managed to lose forty pounds in ten weeks. He continued to preach on Sunday mornings, but most of his other church responsibilities were turned over to Indian leaders.[9]

Although Abraham's condition stabilized, his wife's health deteriorated rapidly. In May 1938 Magdalena began to run a persistent fever and showed signs of yellow jaundice. By June 17 she was confined to a hospital in Chickasha. "It may be Galstone [sic], congested liver or cancer," Becker wrote his friend H. W. Lohrenz. "They do not tell me much on count of my heart trouble, but I found out they want to operate Tuesday. Brother Lohrenz, I am heart broken. The God that helped us so long will not forsake us." Following the surgery to remove three large gallstones, Becker was ecstatic as he reported the results to Lohrenz: "God has heard our prayers beyond expectations." "The doctors are astonished." "They say she may live for years yet." Unfortunately, these early positive signs proved misleading. Magdalena's apparently unlimited supply of reserve energy was overtaxed by a complicated gall and liver ailment.[10]

As news of her worsening condition spread, a steady stream of visitors—Indians and whites—came to Chickasha. Staff at the hospital had never before witnessed such a daily outpouring of love and concern. A group of Comanches maintained a prayer vigil on the hospital grounds. After H. W. Lohrenz visited Mrs. Becker, he published a notice in the *Zionsbote* requesting the prayers of the Mennonite Brethren constituency. On the morning of July 7, the end came, in the presence of her husband and six children. Magdalena looked at all of them and said to the youngest son, twice, "Glenn," but could say no more and died quietly.[11]

The far-reaching impact of Magdalena Becker's life and career was vividly demonstrated in the large attendance at her memorial service and funeral. There were white people from churches in Oklahoma, Kansas, and elsewhere, representatives from other mission stations throughout southwestern Oklahoma, and Mexican Christians from the three mission centers she helped establish. But most noticeably, the Indians came from all directions and from miles around. Some brought tents because of the distance they traveled to reach Post Oak Mission. At the time of Quanah Parker's funeral, Mrs. Becker said never again would there be so many people crowded into their little church. Her prediction was now proved wrong. Approximately 1,500 people attended her funeral on July 10, 1938, more than had witnessed the burial of the nationally-renowned Comanche chief. A large tent, placed adjacent to the mission church, helped accomodate the crowd.

Overflow crowd at funeral service of Magdalena Becker at Post Oak Mission, July 10, 1938. Credit: Courtesy of Glenn Becker

The service began in the morning with Indian tributes and testimonies. James Che-bah-tah was in charge. The funeral service was held in the afternoon, with Rev. H. W. Lohrenz delivering the sermon. A quartet from Post Oak and a group from the Corn Mennonite Brethren Church provided music. Salvador Rivera gave the opening prayer. Herman Asenap reflected on Mrs. Becker's influence: "Us Indians didn't know nothing about Christ. We didn't care to hear nothing about Christ. We didn't care nothing about it. You see today what Mrs. Becker has done. I want to say more but my heart feels so heavy. We Indians, we loved her. She was just like a mother to us. She not only tried to build our character—she tried to build up our spiritual life too. We Indians, dear friends, we feel like Mrs. Becker is one of our Indian people. We love her sincerely." An Indian draped a blanket over Mother Becker's coffin as it was carried to the cemetery. Rev. J. J. Wiebe, pastor of the Corn Mennonite Brethren Church, read Scripture and offered the committal prayer. Then, with many tears, the Comanches bade farewell to the one they had come to love and who had loved them dearly.[12]

The life and career of this remarkable woman—missionary for thirty-seven years, and field matron in the U. S. Civil Service for twenty-eight years—inspired this epitaph on her red granite gravestone: "Sacred to her memory, who at all times and every place gave her strength to the weak, her sympathy to the suffering, her sustenance to the poor, and her heart to God." A. J. Becker memorialized her life as wife and mother by quoting Proverbs 31:28: "She looked well to the way of her household. Her children arise up and call her blessed; her husband also, and he praiseth her." This verse was placed on her tombstone as well.[13]

Change and Transition, 1938-1949

Following his wife's death, Abraham threw himself into his work with almost reckless abandon, as if trying to block the loneliness gnawing inside him. "I am working harder in the mission work than I have for years," he told H. W. Lohrenz. "They all love me and stand by me." Instead of bringing in a guest speaker for their September camp meeting, as was usually done, he took on the task himself, preaching morning and evening three days in succession. He and his "Soul Saving Committee" spent more evenings than usual calling on "sinners" he believed were under conviction. He bought and repaired a little shack near the Lawton mission for the women's sewing circle.

Missionary Becker baptizing a young Comanche boy in a creek, 1938.
Credit: Western History Collections, University of Oklahoma Library

In December Becker wrote Lohrenz that he was busy preparing for four Christmas programs, and doing much writing. "Been up three nights until 5 a. m.," he confided. His schedule became even more hectic during the Christmas season. One Sunday he preached at Post Oak, conducted a baptismal service at Lawton, and participated in an evening program at Richards Spur. The next day he drove 133 miles for three more services. That was followed by a funeral service for a 101-year-old, a woman member of the church. In reporting this event, Becker recalled having baptized a woman two years earlier who was also 101. They had carried her into the water on a bed sheet, and with the help of two men he had successfully and safely immersed her. "She still gives testimonies with much sense in it," he marveled. Concerned about Becker's heavy schedule of activities, Rev. Lohrenz cautioned his friend: "I hope you will not work too hard, but take your rest at least during the night."[1]

Anna Gomez, who had been officially added to the staff, assumed responsibilities for the women's work after Mrs. Becker's death. Walter Gomez, son of Anna and Joe Gomez, and Sam Becker occasionally filled in for Rev. Becker when he could be persuaded to take a little time off. A young niece, Luella Kliewer, came to live with him for awhile, taking care of household duties and helping with the music program. Also, the Indians demonstrated praiseworthy leadership. "They have been so faithful with the Lord's work," Becker observed.[2] It was becoming clear, however, that at age sixty-seven, and with heart trouble, Becker could not carry the load much longer. "I wish so

Joe and Anna Hiebert Gomez, long-time mission workers, and family. Left to right: Joe, Anna, Josephine, Walter, Annadena, Aurara, Joe Jr.   Credit: Courtesy of Glenn Becker

much to have a young missionary couple here as assistant," he told his mission board. There was so much that could be accomplished with the young people he felt, but he was just getting too old to do it. He desired to get a new missionary established on the field and then retire in Lawton near some of his children. He would assist as a volunteer as long as health permitted. He wanted his son Sam to succeed him at Post Oak, but apparently the younger Becker did not feel "called" to the ministry.[3]

The Board of Foreign Missions agreed that a replacement for the work should be found and opened discussions with John S. Dick, former missionary to China. At the same time, the board urged Becker to take steps that would gradually lead to Post Oak becoming a self-sustaining congregation, free of mission board funding and supervision. It was suggested that the church might assume the costs of interpreters, vacation Bible school, and building repairs. "The greatest gain would not consist of saving these small amounts for other purposes," H. W. Lohrenz wrote, "but in leading the church to appreciate its own responsibility and gradually make it self sustaining."[4]

Becker responded that the church had already assumed many of its operational costs. The membership paid the cost of Sunday school supplies, the janitor's salary, fuel for the dining hall and community building, mileage for persons bringing Indians without transportation to church, and recreational events. They contributed funds for associational and camp meetings and communion offerings were designated to support Mennonite Brethren missions world-wide. But he agreed that the church could do more. They were capable of paying vacation Bible school expenses and utility bills. The interpreters' stipend could be dropped. What Post Oak could not do yet, he said, was pay missionary salaries and major building costs. With the growth of the mission in recent years, and the large number of young people, Becker was optimistic the goal of becoming a self-sustaining church would eventually be reached. He believed that under the leadership of an experienced man like John S. Dick, progress toward that objective could continue.[5]

Rev. Dick visited Post Oak in the spring of 1940 and conferred with the missionaries and the Indian church council. Becker and the Indians were almost unanimous in the view that Dick was "just the right man" for the position. One member believed that an Indian should be appointed, and he was anxious to be selected as missionary. According to Becker, the group consensus was that the man was not ready to assume such great responsibilities.[6]

*Post Oak Mission congregation showing large group of young people, circa 1938.
Credit: Western History Collections, University of Oklahoma Libraries.*

In October the Board of Foreign Missions invited the Dicks to take over supervision of the Post Oak mission field. After prolonged deliberation they accepted the position, agreeing to begin in the new year. Dick's salary was set at $800 annually. On January 12, 1941 John and Tina Dick were commissioned for service at a big festival at Post Oak.

Becker planned to remain at Post Oak for a few months of transition occupying a room formerly used as an office. He wished to use the room even after moving to Lawton, so "whenever I come this way I have a place day or night where I can quietly sneek [sic] in for rest and prayer." He did not want to be "intirely [sic] disconnected" from his home of nearly forty years. This particular room held many memories. It was "a room for prayer in our difficulties," and where "we took the Indians that wanted our prayers and help when in trouble or grief." It was where, on many late nights, Magdalena had written her field matron reports. After her death, it became his "most pressious [sic] place under the sun." Many tears were shed there; and "many prayers were answered there." He had closed the room off from the rest of the house and built a door to the outside, so he would not be in the way of the new occupants. However, he soon discovered how dearly John and Tina Dick, and their daughter Wilma, cherished their privacy. The kindly, but deeply disappointed, veteran missionary gave up the idea of keeping his room and moved into a house he had purchased in Lawton.[7]

Not only was it difficult for Becker to leave Post Oak and "his Indians," the Comanches also had trouble adjusting to the change. Following the beloved "White Beard" was not an easy assignment for the new worker either. Rev. Dick had twenty years of missionary experience, but little understanding of Comanche culture and history. He found it difficult to relate to his Indian congregation. Becker advised that not "too many changes be made at the beginning," and then only in cooperation with the nine-member church council. He believed that after the Indians and the new missionary got to know each other better, "things should go in harmony." But six months later Becker was grieved to report that "things do not go well between Dicks and the Indians." Changes had been made too quickly, he feared, before a "heart connection" had taken place. Both sides needed patience; it had taken him fifteen years, he said, to learn how to work with the Comanches. Becker deliberately spent little time at Post Oak "so the Indians get more in close touch with their missionary and not hang around me." He still believed the Indians wanted to work together in a good relationship with the Dicks.[8]

After moving to Lawton, Becker spent much of his time assisting at the Mexican mission. Salvador Rivera, a graduate of a Bible training school in Texas, was appointed missionary to the Mexicans at Lawton and Richards Spur. The mission board kept Becker on salary to superintend the field, paying him $300 from the mission treasury and $300 a year from the pension fund.[9] The Mexican work caused Becker some heartaches. Interpersonal problems developed with Mrs. Rivera, and there were differences over how monies should be spent. After a lifetime of living on a shoestring budget, Becker was very frugal, even during the more prosperous World War II years when the mission budget increased. He was deeply attached to Salvador and praised him as a great preacher. When the mission board refused to grant the young minister ordination, due to a divorce before his conversion, Rivera resigned. Despite some problems, it was generally agreed that Rivera had been an effective pioneer worker among his own people at the Post Oak Mexican Mission in Lawton.[10]

Magdalena's death left A. J. Becker a very lonely man. He told friends that he had always had people around him and could not get used to being alone. "My home is just the walls to me," he lamented to H. W. Lohrenz. Thus it was not totally surprising to his family and close friends when he informed them of his plans to marry Katharina (Tina) Poetker. This fifty-four-year-old woman had been born in Russia and lived in Oklahoma and Texas before moving to Canada. The couple conducted courtship through letters between Oklahoma and Canada. They had never seen each other until he picked her up at the Union Depot in St. Louis, Missouri to bring her to Lawton for their wedding. To help recognize each other they agreed that she would wear a white corsage and he would wear a white rosebud in his lapel and be carrying a cane. The wedding ceremony took place on November 30, 1941 in the presence of all the Becker children, grandchildren, and "adopted" children. The latter consisted of David C. Peters, Anna Gomez, and Salvador Rivera. Rev. J. J. Wiebe read the wedding vows. He likened their experience to the Old Testament story of Isaak and Rebecca. Through prayer they "found each other; and he loved her and was comforted." By all reports, Tina also loved A. J. and was likewise comforted.[11]

At Post Oak, meanwhile, missionary Dick was gradually becoming more sensitive to Indian ways, creating a basis for mutual understanding and better relations. After a year on the field Dick remarked that they had "settled down. . . and here we hope to stay till the end of our days."[12] On the morning of March 19, 1942 Rev. Dick faced a full day of activities. A work day to clean up the cemetery had been scheduled and in the afternoon he was to speak at a neighboring mission. He noted that he felt slightly ill and was concerned about keeping his appointments. Determined to get much of the cleanup done in the morning, he reportedly became agitated when his parishioners showed up on "Indian time." [13] Later, while helping burn some grass, he suddenly fell to the ground, dead of an apparent heart attack.

Dick's death was a great shock to the people of Post Oak and the Mennonite constituency. Herman Asenap, who was by his side when he died, said that missionary Dick "gave his life for the Indian people." That a bond, or "heart connection," had developed between the Comanches and the missionary family was demonstrated at a farewell service for Mrs. Dick and daughter Wilma. They were showered with gifts, including several shawls and a beautiful quilt sewn by members of the Magdalena Circle. Rev. Dick's body was returned to Reedley, California for burial, with the Becker Funeral Home handling the arrangements. Later, a marker in his memory was placed on the spot in the cemetery where he had fallen. [14]

The Board of Foreign Missions quickly suggested a new missionary couple: Clarence and Edna Balzer Fast. Originally from Corn, Rev. Fast was a teacher at Zoar Academy in Inman, Kansas. He was acquainted with Post Oak, having spent two summers teaching in the vacation Bible school program. Becker met with the Indian leadership committee to discuss the possible appointment of Fast. Sam No Hand wanted Becker to come back. Abe Hoahwah said, "I want somebody that can teach us to sing. I want a good musician as well as a good preacher." Felix Koweno noted that the appointment of a missionary was a very important matter and needed careful consideration. "This line of work, especially with the Indian people, is a very hard problem," he said. Koweno seemed to have reservations about calling another white missionary. "The Indian people can see in the Indian way better than the white. Have Brother and Sister Fast felt the call of God?" Following their deliberations, the Indian leaders voted to support the appointment of the Fasts. [15]

On June 14, 1942 the Post Oak church bade farewell to Tina and Wilma Dick and formally welcomed the Fasts to their new ministry. Felix Koweno, James Che-bah-tah, and Herman Asenap spoke on behalf of the Comanche members and Rev. Becker delivered the sermon. [16]

Missionary Fast got off to a good start. He already knew many of the young people by name and had good rapport with them. As Becker had recommended, he strengthened the programs for the large number of children and youth in the church. He persuaded several young Comanches to get their high school education at Corn Bible Academy, a Mennonite Brethren school about sixty miles from Indiahoma. Fast was effective with adults too. Seventeen persons were baptized during his ministry, including To-Pay, the last surviving wife of Quanah Parker. He initiated a bus service for those without means of transportation. The first mission bus was a remodeled milk wagon; the second, a converted beer truck. Attendance, which had been lagging, more than doubled with the introduction of the bus service.[17] There was deep regret and disappointment in fall 1944 when Fast announced that due to his wife's ill health he was leaving the field.

Post Oak was once again without a missionary and pastor. This time no replacement was available, so J. J. Wiebe, recently retired from the pastorate at Corn, and a member of the mission board, was appointed to serve on an interim basis. Becker was deeply concerned about Fast's sudden departure. Too many changes in a short time were pulling the work down, he feared. Fortunately, because of Corn's long connection with Post Oak, the Indians knew the gentle, soft-spoken Rev. Wiebe had a big heart for the mission and its people. Together, they would pull through this crisis.[18]

There were more changes at Lawton as well. In January 1944 Walter and Lois Gomez assumed responsibility for the Mexican ministry. They were recruited from Minneapolis, where they had started an urban ministry while attending Northwestern Bible College. An aggressive youth program, meetings for women, and an expanded church bus service into south Lawton stimulated great interest and increased attendance. Gomez was a dynamic speaker in both Spanish and English; Lois Gomez was a talented pianist and a trained Sunday school worker. Using a mobile loudspeaker system, the mission work was expanded to several outlying work camp areas.

A gifted fund raiser, Rev. Gomez personally raised the money for the speaker system and a piano. He had other ambitious plans for expansion of the mission program. The Board of Foreign Missions, however, fearing private fund raising might reduce contributions to the overall mission budget, adopted a policy prohibiting such activity by missionaries.

There were some ruffled feelings in the transition from the Riveras to the Gomezes, but Rev. Becker's spirits were lifted by the presence of the new missionary couple. He was frequently part of the Sunday morning preaching team; Gomez preached in Spanish and he gave an English sermon.

Due to various circumstances, including the restrictive fund raising policy and the fact that many of the migrant workers were leaving the Lawton area, Walter Gomez asked to be released from the station after two years of service. His ultimate goal was to preach the gospel to his father's people in Mexico. The young couple left Lawton in June 1946; they subsequently established the Mexican Mission Ministries.[19]

Because of population shifts the Post Oak Mexican Mission began to focus its work on a racially mixed population at the southeastern edge of Lawton. This "shantytown" area, known as Lawton View Addition, consisted of poor blacks, Indians, Mexicans, and whites, with the latter the most numerous. Rather than busing people to the mission, Rev. Becker recommended the church be relocated in Lawton View. He purchased two lots there, donated them to the Mennonite Brethren conference, and offered to pay part of the building costs for a church at the new location. He had a little income from the farm he had homesteaded near Fairview and from land he had purchased in the Big Pasture area many years earlier. "Since I am too old and feeble to help much in church," he wrote, "I feel to do something finantionaly [sic] and do it gladly." The mission board immediately accepted his recommendation and generous offer.[20]

With manual labor from Becker and Harry Bartel, a mission worker, and the usual reliable volunteers from Corn, a small chapel was erected by October 1946. Soon after the lease on the original property was sold and the mission building moved to the new site for use as a residence. Lawton View Mission, as it was now called, worked multiculturally with Mexicans, Indians, and whites. It was the only non-black church in the Addition. Blacks had attended Post Oak Mission in the early years, but Becker said there were six churches serving the "Coloreds" in Lawton View, and he did not want to engage in "sheep stealing." Occasionally Bible classes were held with black children.[21]

The Mennonite Brethren now had the biggest urban mission in Lawton. Becker called it the "most promising field our conference has." "These are very poor people," he informed the mission board. "And God made so many of them and he himself was poor." Needed for this field, he advised, were experienced, ordained workers who loved the poor. Since the departure of Walter Gomez, he confessed being "very much worried . . . concerning Lawton View Mission."[22]

Temporary or short-term missionaries could not hold the work together, he feared. Some of the current workers were "gone too much of the time." There were problems that needed attention: friction between and among families in the church, and violation of church rules against movie attendance, smoking, and use of snuff. "Weak ones" drift away "when they are not continually taken care of," Becker explained. He had urged the station missionaries not to take their vacation in August because it was too hot for him to fill in for them then. They had gone anyway, even taking the church van for their trip. Weakened by illness, made worse by an extremely hot summer, the discouraged and weary missionary asked the mission board to accept his resignation. "I do not fit in and have nothing to say anyway or can not, except say yes."[23]

Two months later Becker again submitted his resignation, stating that his doctor had forbidden him to do any work. Since the Harry Bartels were being reassigned to Colombia, he suggested some possible replacements. The Bartels had done good work, he said, but repeated his plea for an experienced, ordained missionary for this difficult field. On November 12, A. E. Janzen informed Becker that the Board of Foreign Missions reluctantly accepted his resignation and released him from all responsibilities at Lawton. Frank Nickel was appointed as the new station missionary. Nickel was inexperienced, but Becker was pleased that arrangements would be made for him to be ordained by the Buhler (Kansas) Mennonite Brethren Church.[24]

Becker's concerns about the frequent turnover of missionaries at Post Oak were lessened by the appointment in 1945 of Dietrich J. (Dick) and Linda Gerbrandt. Graduates of Tabor College, a Mennonite Brethren institution in Hillsboro, Kansas, they visited with Becker and the Post Oak church council during the Christmas break of 1944-45. The Indians made it clear they wanted to play a major role in the selection process. After the visit, Becker reported to the mission board that the Gerbrandts "made a very good empression [sic] on the Indians and myself."[25] The Comanches apparently made a good impression on the visiting couple; on June 6, 1945 the Gerbrandts were formally welcomed to the field with the usual daylong festivities. As the elder statesman of Mennonite Brethren missions, Becker gave Gerbrandt the same advice he had given his predecessors: "Do nothing new of importance the first year, and then with the Church Council and the Church." It takes years "to know the Indians and know how to work with them," he counseled, so "you must learn patience."[26]

The Gerbrandts were not only blessed with patience, they had other attributes that served them well as missionaries. Linda Wiens Gerbrandt, born in China of missionary parents, had developed a sensitivity toward other cultures. Her husband Dick, unlike many missionaries of that time, had a lively interest in Indian history and culture. He wished to see the Comanches converted to Christianity without the destruction of their language and cultural heritage.

The Bureau of Indian Affairs during the Franklin D. Roosevelt Administration had adopted a more enlightened policy toward Indians. Under commissioner John Collier the government moved away from the earlier view that "Indianness" had to be destroyed to assure progress. Collier was determined to promote a sense of pride among the Indians. Historians and ethnologists were encouraged to write about Indian culture and achievements for use in Indian schools. Linguists were employed to reduce native languages to a written form. Under the Oklahoma Indian Welfare Act, passed by Congress in 1936, Indians were encouraged to re-establish tribal governments as "instruments of progress" for native peoples. Although the reforms of Collier's "Indian New Deal" did not end their economic problems or the widespread discrimination they faced in Oklahoma, it did result in a new appreciation of the uniqueness of Indian culture.[27]   The Gerbrandts, like the Beckers before them, apparently recognized the need to gain an understanding of Comanche culture in order to relate meaningfully to them.

Rev. Gerbrandt had ambitious plans to expand the outreach of Post Oak Mission. His first project, implemented in fall 1946, was to establish a Bible training school for adults. Courses were taught twice a week in church history, Bible history, Sunday school pedagogy, and aspects of Indian culture. In 1948 a Comanche language class was offered by Elliot Canoge, a linguist with the Wycliffe Bible Translators. Canoge was engaged in field work in southwestern Oklahoma as part of a project to translate the Bible into the Comanche language. He had produced two Comanche primers to teach Indians to read the written words of their language. While at Post Oak he translated into written form many of the songs used by local Comanche Christians.[28]

A second major new undertaking was the establishment of an accredited parochial school for elementary students. The idea was to provide the Indians with Christian training along with the state's required curriculum. It was believed that in a more sheltered environment the children could be thoroughly grounded in the faith and would, therefore, be less prone to "backslide" into the ways of the "world." It appears the church was having trouble retaining its youth. The plan received the endorsement of the missionary council and a number of Indian leaders. A. J. Becker had reservations, which he voiced to A. E. Janzen and P. R. Lange, chair of the Board of Foreign Missions. He had been president of the Indiahoma school board and knew the costs of running a school. The expenses of a new building, teaching staff, and purchase of a bus and supplies made this "too big a bite" for the Mennonite Brethren Conference, he believed. He favored a Bible School, but not a "Credited Indian school."[29]   After hearing his views, Lange apparently got the impression that Becker and Gerbrandt did not "get along too well."   But Becker quickly dispelled that view by declaring he considered "Brother and Sister Gerbrandt . . . very good missionaries;" theirs was only an honest disagreement over the school issue.[30] The mission board sided with Gerbrandt. Janzen informed Becker that although they respected his views, the members of the board had voted to open a school in Indiahoma. If for some reason it did not meet with success, they could close it down and use the facilities for other purposes.[31]

The mission board authorized the purchase of land in Indiahoma, and construction of a school building began in 1948. In September 1948, classes for the first four grades were held in the club house at Post Oak Mission. Ruth Wiens was the first teacher; there were twenty-eight pupils. The following year classes were held in the basement of the new building under construction in Indiahoma.

In 1949 Herman Neufeld of Buhler, Kansas was appointed as missionary at Post Oak Mission, freeing Gerbrandt to become a full-time teacher and principal of the school. By 1951 the school building and an apartment building for teachers had been completed and classes were offered through the eighth grade. Enrollment in the early years ranged from fifty to over seventy pupils. Several Indians, including Edith Kassanavoid and Flora Roach, were employed as cooks in the school cafeteria.[32] Sarah Grunau supervised the school lunch program. Gerbrandt urged that a high school be added because he had observed that "almost all young Indians are lost for the church during their high school years."[33] This proposal was not approved.

Another venture undertaken by the Gerbrandts—one that lasted eight years—was the establishment of a home for destitute Indian children. The Gerbrandts discovered that six children, wards of the court, needed care. The missionary couple, with five children of their own, agreed to provide a home for them. Ranging in age from thirteen months to thirteen years, the Gerbrandts housed, fed, and raised them as their own children. Eventually a house was purchased in Indiahoma to be used as an "orphanage." Here the children were cared for by two volunteer matrons, Sarah Grunau and Eva Schmidt; however, the Gerbrandts continued to serve as their "parents." Members of Post Oak Mission supplied groceries to help defray expenses. This obviously worthy cause received no subsidy from the mission board. In fact, in 1949 that body directed the Gerbrandts "to make different arrangements" for the children's care "in order to effect the discontinuation of the orphanage as soon as possible." The board believed that "the General Mission program together with the newly established school at Indiahoma constitutes the limit of our possibilities in this particular field."[34]

The childrens' home closed in 1955 with the departure of the Gerbrandts. By that time two of the Indian girls had married; the other children were returned to their mother who, in the interim, had married and established a stable home. One of the Gerbrandt's "adopted" girls married Kenneth Sauppitty, a member of the Post Oak Mission Church who became chairman of the Comanche tribal government. In recognition of their contributions to the welfare of Indian people, Dick and Linda Gerbrandt were given the signal honor of being inducted into the Quahada band of the Comanche tribe. [35]

As a result of staff realignments in 1953, Gerbrandt was transferred from the school program to supervise the Post Oak Mission extension work. A male musical group known as the "Friendly Five Quintet" was organized to give programs in local churches and Mennonite communities. Evangelistic teams were sent as far away as Arizona Indian reservations, and the mission's religious programming at Fort Sill Indian School was placed under Gerbrandt's supervision. Also, Max Pahcheka, a star athlete and graduate of Tabor College, with his wife Lizzie, were commissioned as missionaries to the Shoshoni Indians on the Wind River Reservation. The Post Oak congregation committed itself to provide funds for this missionary outreach.[36]

Missionaries Herman and Ann Neufeld, recent Tabor College graduates, initially proceeded along the paths carved out by their predecessors. Soon, however, some major changes took place that affected the future course of Post Oak. The Neufelds were assigned to implement steps that would result in the mission be-coming a self-sustaining congregation in the Southern District of the Mennonite Brethren Church Conference.

The End of the Becker Era

A. J. Becker might have used the words from a favorite spiritual, "Sometimes I'm up, sometimes I'm down," to characterize his health and spirits after resigning from his supervisory role in late 1947. In January 1948 he and his wife entered a Texas clinic for a series of medical tests. Even in illness he retained his sense of humor. Writing about a tube his doctors had inserted into his body, he said, "I don't mind as long as it is not thicker than a water hose."[1] His condition improved somewhat as a result of the treatments received, but he remained under strict medical care.

On Decoration Day, May 30, Becker's son Bill took him to Post Oak to observe the Indians decorating the cemetery. Rev. Gerbrandt hooked up a microphone and loudspeaker, allowing Becker to speak to the Indians from the car. He recalled the many times they had worked together beautifying the graves of their loved ones. He again told them that they had "very good missionaries in the Gerbrandts and Anna Gomez," and urged his Comanche friends "to stand by them." This visit to the old mission site was a great boost to his morale. "I was so happy to be once more with my Indians that love me so," he reported to the chairman of the mission board. He optimistically looked forward to the time when he could resume some visitation work among them.[2]

It soon appeared that this hope would not be realized. In August 1948 Glenn Becker informed the mission board that his father had suffered a severe heart attack, followed a few days later by two strokes. He was confined to bed with no visitors allowed. "He would still like to visit the lost, distribute literature, encourage the Christian and play with the children—even now expressing these desires," the son reported. The news of Becker's illness was given to delegates of the General Conference of the Mennonite Brethren Church, meeting in Mountain Lake, Minnesota. It resulted in an outpouring of prayer and messages of support for the celebrated veteran missionary. Becker's condition stabilized more quickly than expected, and he soon showed remarkable improvement. Just as prayer had rescued him from a herd of wild longhorns some fifty years earlier, he now believed prayer had staved off death and allowed him a few more years to finish his assignments on earth.[3]

Within a few months Becker was pecking away on his old "German-English" typewriter, composing letters and preparing an article for the *Mennonite Encyclopedia*. Off and on, with the help of his children, he worked on a history of Post Oak Mission.[4]

By winter 1949 he was ready to get back in harness to look after the interests of his "baby," the Lawton View Mission. Because of his illnesses, and the delay in ordaining missionary Frank Nickel, the sacraments of baptism and communion had not been administered in two years. This neglect, he wrote the mission board, "belittles the work here." He reiterated his contention that Lawton View was potentially "the greatest Mission Field we have in the U. S." He gently chided the board by reminding them that this mission to Mexicans, Indians, and whites was "a child" that needed to be nursed and cared for, or it would die. He informed the members that he was well enough to once again officiate at ceremonies that required an ordained minister.[5]

Although Becker maintained contact with Post Oak Mission, he increasingly became an outside observer rather than active participant. He was aware of the school's struggles to gain accreditation, the problems with one of the deacons, and the desire of Indian members to have a greater voice in things. But these were problems he was no longer expected to solve, although his counsel was still sought.

There was one issue on which Becker refused to stay on the sidelines—the proposed confiscation of the Post Oak Mission property by the Fort Sill army base. In the early 1950s the Department of Defense announced plans to acquire 38,000 acres of land west of Fort Sill to expand the post's artillery and guided missile range. The proposed acquisition included Post Oak Mission and the cemetery where over seven hundred Comanches were buried. When he heard of the proposal, Rev. Becker was shocked. Everything they had worked for over the past fifty years would be lost. The government was prepared to callously disregard the solemn pledges made to Quanah Parker personally and to the Comanches as a tribe at the turn of the century. The thought of losing the sacred and historic cemetery where Magdalena, an infant daughter, and many Comanche friends were buried, was almost more than he could bear. The Board of Foreign Missions and the Mennonite constituency must vigorously protest the proposed land grab, he wrote A. E. Janzen. He urged a letter writing campaign to Oklahoma's congressional delegation, though he recognized it would be hard to overcome the influence of powerful interests at Fort Sill and in Lawton. He pledged to give his "Last Strength even if it kills me," to save Post Oak.[6]

Becker had a strong ally in Neda Parker Birdsong, the widowed and aging daughter of Chief Parker. Included in Fort Sill's proposed new line of fire was the famous Star House. Neda had refurbished a portion of the twelve-room structure and lived there alone with her memories. Her father and grandmother, Cynthia Ann Parker, were buried at nearby Post Oak Cemetery. This Carlisle-educated daughter had composed the epitaph carved onto Quanah's monument: "Resting here until day breaks and shadows fall and darkness disappears is Quanah Parker, last chief of the Comanches." The picturesque spot where the chief and his mother were buried was at the highest point of the cemetery so that their two monuments rose conspicuously above the prairie landscape, the mountains appearing as a rampart on the north. Other Parker family members were buried there, and all through the cemetery were the mounded graves of Comanches with names and birthdates going back to a tepee-dwelling, buffalo hunting, Stone Age culture. On October 28, 1952 Birdsong called on Becker and the two agreed to join forces to oppose the Fort Sill expansion plan. They also agreed to aid other opposition groups, such as the cattlemen who held Indian leases, and the towns of Cache and Indiahoma. Becker told Birdsong that although he was "past 80 years" and could not do much, "I will do all I can."[7]

Actually Becker did more than he should have, considering his age and the state of his health. "I am always dizzy," he confessed. "I can not write anymore." Since his wife Tina had difficulty writing in English, he dictated fifteen letters to a neighbor, voicing his opposition to the expansion plan. He mailed them to congressmen and others who might be able to influence the decision. By November he was forced to use a wheelchair. Still he pressed on, consumed with the fear of losing his beloved mission grounds. "I have been thinking day and night and praying day and night of how we can save Post Oak Mission and the cemetery," one of his letters to A. E. Janzen stated. He had given his life there and wanted to be buried with Magdalena and his Comanches: "The Indians loved Us so much, They called us Mother and Father."[8]

Janzen responded to Becker's letters with assurances that the mission board would do all it could to prevent the government taking the land. They too were frightened by the prospect of losing the Mennonite Brethren's first foreign mission site. "The Lord will help us if it is his will," he declared.[9]

As it turned out, there was more opposition to expansion plans for Fort Sill than the Pentagon expected. Senator Robert S. Kerr's contact person in Lawton, Miles Reber, reported: "All ranchers and farmers raising the dickens about the proposal and having school house meetings, etc."[10] Of critical importance was the opposition of the Interior Department, backed by nature lovers and conservationsts, who wanted to keep the area part of the Wichita Mountains Wildlife Refuge. As a result of the uproar over the expansion proposal, the army decided to temporarily drop its plans. In the meantime, they would devise a "divide and conquer" approach against their opponents, a technique successfully used against the American Indians since the days of George Washington.

By December, 1952 Rev. Becker was rarely strong enough to leave the house. He greatly appreciated the visits of his children and grandchildren who lived in the area. He took great pride in the accomplishments of his five sons and one daughter. All had graduated from college, five had master's degrees from the University of Oklahoma. Dan served as the principal of Lawton High School; Bill was a profes-

A.J. Becker family in the chapel of the Becker Funeral Home, Lawton, OK., circa 1948. Left to right: seated, William, Abraham, Herwanna, Daniel. Standing, Samuel, Glenn, Peter Credit: Courtesy of Glenn Becker

sor at Cameron College; Herwanna taught school at Cache, and would later be a professor of English at colleges in Weatherford and Edmond, Oklahoma; Pete and Glenn owned and operated a large funeral home in Lawton; Sam was an engineer in Oklahoma City. What pleased him more than their educational and professional accomplishments was the fact that they and their spouses were active church members.[11]

On January 10, 1953 missionary Becker suffered another cerebral hemorrhage. All realized that this time the end was near; Abraham's last strength had been expended in the struggle to save the historic Post Oak site. The ever-faithful Anna Gomez kept vigil at his bedside. She had stood with Magdalena and Rev. Becker beside many deathbeds over the years and was almost like a member of their family. On January 15, a few hours before dawn, A. J. Becker breathed his last breath.

A memorial service was held at the First Baptist Church in Lawton on January 17, followed by the burial service at Post Oak Mission and cemetery. The spacious Baptist Church, where several of the Becker sons were members, could comfortably accomodate a large crowd on a wintry January day. H. Tom Wiles, pastor of the church, and P. R. Lange, chair of the Board of Foreign Missions, conducted the service. A. E. Janzen, executive secretary of the board, eulogized Becker as a man who was judged great in the eyes of God, in the eyes of the Indians, and in the eyes of the many whose lives had been touched by his ministry. He recalled Becker's love for his Indians, "his sympathetic and constant concern about their welfare, his self-denying toil in their behalf, his unceasing struggle together with them to raise their standard of life, and his intercessory service with the government agencies to safeguard [their] interests." An example of enduring, sacrificial love was the Becker legacy, Janzen declared. Missionary Becker loved his God, his Indians, his church: there lay his greatness as a pioneer Mennonite missionary. Herman Asenap spoke a tribute for the Indians, as he had at Magdalena Becker's funeral. He expressed the Comanches' great love and respect for Becker. "Father Becker" had come to work among them and "became one of us." He would never be forgotten. Archie Kliewer, a nephew and music instructor at Tabor College, sang a solo.

Rev. Herman Neufeld conducted the service at the mission cemetery. A large crowd of Indians, Mexicans, and whites gathered to see the beloved missionary buried next to his wife Magdalena. Rev. Becker had requested an "Indian burial," with the mourners witnessing the closing of the grave. Pallbearers were converts and leaders in the church: Robert Coffee, Max Pahcheka, James Che-bah-tah, Felix Koweno, Pete Coffee, and Dick Codopony. As scoops of sod tumbled over the casket and formed a mound over the grave, the final chapter in the Becker era of Post Oak Mission history came to a close.[12]

A.J. Becker with the pulpit Bible he used throughout his ministry at Post Oak Mission, circa 1952. Credit: Archives & Manuscripts Division of the Oklahoma Historical Society

Post Oak Under Fire: The Fort Sill Expansion Controversy

T wo issues dominated the history of Post Oak Mission in the 1950s: the threat to, and eventual loss of the mission grounds, and the change of status from a "foreign" mission project to a self-administered Mennonite Brethren church. As feared by the Mennonites and the Indiahoma and Cache area Comanches, the army revived its plans to expand Fort Sill's artillery and guided missile range. This time they had a clever strategy to undercut opposition groups. Rumors were spread that if the army could not acquire additional land it would move the post outside the state. This threat galvanized the support of Lawton's Chamber of Commerce and city officials in surrounding communities. Business interests flooded the Oklahoma delegation in Congress with telegrams and letters. Furthermore, the Defense Department managed to placate the champions of the 10,500 acre wildlife refuge with the promise to use this tract only as a buffer zone, thus protecting it from annexation.   Under the revised plan most of the army's high-powered explosives would fall on "generally useless" private land which it proposed to buy south of the refuge. The "useless" land selected for pulverization by Cold War missiles included the Post Oak Mission and cemetery, the Star House, and other Comanche homes. A concern and willingness to protect the welfare of the buffalos and long-horned cattle did not, it appeared, extend to the Comanche people or their historic sites.

The Comanches had little influence in Washington during the Termination Policy era of the 1950's; the Mennonites had even less. The army's offer to remove the cemetery and pay for the mission buildings and Star House was supposed to make everything right. "If we were in a war where boys were giving their lives," said Neda Birdsong, "and I were asked to give my father's house I would walk out of this door without one word. But in a time of peace it seems to me they could take a little more thought and make some better plans."[1]

Correspondence of the Mennonite Brethren mission board shows that by spring 1955 they had become reconciled to the harsh fact that their property would likely be annexed. After A. J. Becker's death, no Mennonite individual or organized group emerged to lead the battle for the preservation of the Post Oak mission site. The board tentatively agreed that if forced to move, the mission and cemetery would be relocated in Indiahoma near the mission school. In a letter to Senator Robert S. Kerr of Oklahoma, the board's executive secretary requested that certain stipulations be honored if the expansion bill passed. Firstly, the cemetery should be relocated intact at government expense and continue to be called the "Post Oak Mission Cemetery;" secondly, proper compensation should be awarded the denomination to purchase property and develop new facilities for the mission. [2]

Even before expansion of the army post became an issue, some missionaries and board members had broached the idea of moving the church into Indiahoma where a number of the members lived. The Post Oak site, under this scenario, would be used for camp meetings, baptisms, and other special activities. The Indiahoma location, it was suggested, would eliminate the need and expense of busing members to church. Rev. Becker had opposed the idea, preferring the quiet, peaceful atmosphere of the rural location.

In 1954, after the first scare of an army takeover had subsided, the mission board unveiled sweeping proposals for the future course of Post Oak. The major recommendation called for transfer of mission operations to the local Indian membership. This was in keeping with a new philosophy and strategy in all the denomination's mission enterprises. The proposals for change of status were included in a report prepared by John B. Toews, newly-appointed mission administrator, and A. E. Janzen, following an inspection tour of Post Oak, Indiahoma, and Lawton View. In a session with the Indian members of the church council, with no missionaries present, it had become clear that the Indians believed they "should be given greater consideration in decisions and administration." Toews and Janzen reported that the Indians were concerned that decisions were often made arbitrarily and independently by the missionaries without consultation with the Indian members. Based on the views and wishes of the Indian leaders and other observations, the two men concluded a new policy should be established for the "administration and promotion of the spiritual as well as organizational work" at the mission.

Janzen and Toews proposed several steps to be implemented over a period of time. For convenience and efficiency, mission activities should be centered in Indiahoma on property already owned by the denomination. That would also provide an opportune time to transfer the church administration and property to the Comanche congregation. An Indian pastor, chosen in cooperation with the church council, should be appointed. Title to the property would be transferred to the Indian Mennonite Brethren Church as soon as the congregation was prepared to assume the costs of supporting a pastor and maintaining the property. The residence occupied by Joe and Anna Gomez at Post Oak should be moved to Indiahoma for their use. Eventually it could become the church parsonage. The cemetery would remain at Post Oak and the Board of Foreign Missions would continue to own the Post Oak land and other buildings. A tenant could be located on the property to maintain the cemetery and other grounds, and produce some revenue from the pasture land. The Post Oak compound would still be used for camp meetings, church retreats, recreational activities, and other "occasions of Christian character."[3]

Staff re-assignments were also contemplated under the proposals to the board. Herman and Ann Neufeld would be moved to Indiahoma to implement the transfer plans. Thereafter they would be assigned to the Lawton View Mission. Dick and Linda Gerbrandt would be assigned to a field yet to be determined. Their responsibilities for the extension work would be assumed by a teacher from Post Oak Mission School.[4]

The mission board approved the recommended changes in principle; however, word was soon received that the Post Oak property was once again in danger of seizure by the U. S. Army. Nevertheless, some of the changes, with certain modifications, were implemented in summer 1955. It was decided that Herman Neufeld and Dan Petker of Lawton View should exchange fields, with the latter now charged with the transfer of responsibilities to the Native Americans. The move was made at this time because Petker could also fill the job of principal at the Indian school in Indiahoma, which was without an administrator. The Gerbrandts were assigned to a mission field in Mexico; they left Indiahoma on August 28. The relocation of the mission church was put on hold until Post Oak's future was determined.[5]

The relocation issue was exceedingly traumatic for the Indians. James Che-bah-tah expressed the concerns of the Post Oak members in a letter to Janzen: "We appreciate what the mennonite brethren [sic] has done for our people. . . . More than fifty years we have been struggling against various obstacles in an attempt to proclaim the gospel from this place of worship. . . . In spite of all the shifting about the Lord knew the way which we should go, and he has abundantly [sic] blessed. . . . Now again the military expanse program has come up again and that means we will surrender our place of worship and also our cemetary [sic] and it becomes a burden to our people. . . ." He requested that a member of the board be sent to "enlighten" them on their future.[6] Missionary Herman Neufeld reported that, "An untold amount of confusion and dissatisfaction is prevailing in the minds of the local Indians." Those who were being relocated were at a loss to know what to do. To move the graves of their ancestors, he stated, and to worship in a new environment would be a severe adjustment for them.[7]

By fall 1955 the rumored Fort Sill expansion plan had been officially authorized. The Comanches had been compelled to move many times in their history, but this was the first time they were faced with the forced removal of their dead. Over a period of almost sixty years the Post Oak Cemetery had become a sacred religious site. To disturb the bodies of their ancestors was unthinkable. To do so, Quanah Parker's wife To-Pay said, would be a "bad omen." The Mennonite Brethren mission board faced the dilemma of trying to reconcile the Indians to the inevitable. What the Indians needed was the counsel and guiding hand of a "Father Becker" to help them cope with this crisis. The current missionary was too new to fill that role. Ultimately it fell to A. E. Janzen, executive secretary of the mission board, to convince them the battle was lost, and that together they must select a new location for their church and cemetery on the best terms possible.

The breakthrough came when Rev. Janzen was able to convince the Indian elders that there was scriptural support for moving the grave of a loved one. During a Sunday service at Post Oak, Janzen read selections from the books of Genesis, Exodus, and Joshua, recounting the death and burial of Joseph in Egypt and subsequent removal of his bones to Canaan by the great patriarch Moses. Hearing this biblical precedent for moving graves resolved the matter, according to Janzen. Indian Christians, he explained, "have an unequivocal faith that what the Bible says is decisive" and to act upon biblical precedent was right and proper. They were now resigned to removal of the graves to a new location. However, it would be some time before agreement could be reached on where to relocate the cemetery.[8]

During the spring and summer of 1956 the United States Army Corps of Engineers and the Mennonite Brethren mission board in Hillsboro, Kansas conducted drawn-out negotiations over the relocation agreement. Meanwhile, the board purchased sixteen lots in Indiahoma for the possible site of a new church building. It had been decided that the old mission church could not be safely moved to another site. The board also took an option on sixty acres of land adjoining the Indiahoma school property on which to relocate the cemetery.[9] Henry Wiebe, a building contractor from Corn, prepared blueprints and cost estimates for a new church.

On May 25, 1956 Janzen conducted a public meeting in Indiahoma to discuss possible sites for a relocated cemetery. People with family members buried at Post Oak were given opportunity to express their opinions. William J. Becker, oldest surviving member of the A. J. Becker family, read a statement representing the family's views. It was their firm belief that the long-term interests of the Comanches, the whites, and the Parker and Becker families would be served best by keeping the cemetery intact as a unit. They saw the Post Oak school as a "unifying center of activity," and recommended that the cemetery and church be located near the school at Indiahoma. The Post Oak Mission Council had also indicated "a sincere desire to keep this unity of School, Church, Cemetery, and Community." [10]

During the discussion, four possible locations were proposed: two on the west side of Indiahoma and two on the east. It was clear that mission officials favored a site located one-half mile west of the school. Not only did they hold an option to buy land there, they had asked Alton Wiebe, principal of the Indian school, to prepare blueprints for a cemetery on those grounds. Another group presented drawings for a location on the eastern edge of town. Following a lengthy discussion and a prayer by Jim Che-bah-tah, those eligible were asked to indicate their preference by ballot. Twenty-five people voted for the site favored by the mission board; ten voted to locate the cemetery immediately adjacent to the schoolground on the west; ten favored the site on the east edge of town; two favored a location three miles east of Indiahoma. Although consensus had not been reached, it was clear that a strong majority of those present favored a location on the west side of town.[11]

In the following months a number of Indians voiced opposition to the locations on the west side of Indiahoma because the land was owned by whites. Seeking to accomodate the Indians, Janzen supported efforts to acquire a 160-acre grant of unoccupied Indian land near Cache where the trading post and subagency office had once stood. This site could then be used for a cemetery and mission operations. In a letter to the agency in Anadarko, Janzen pointed out the Indians' concern that the cemetery be located on Indian land. Furthermore, since they were being forced to give up other historic sites associated with Quanah Parker and his people, the Indians wanted the new location to tie in historically with early Comanche history in Oklahoma. The proposal to grant the land to the Mennonites was rejected; however, the government did offer to set aside enough land for a Comanche cemetery at the Cache site.[12] It was becoming clear that because of the diversity of interests and pressures it would be difficult to keep the Post Oak Cemetery intact as a unit.

On June 29, 1956 J. Lee Hogue Jr., Chief, Real Estate Division, Corps of Engineers, informed Janzen that their office had determined that fair market value of the 158.6-acre tract owned by the Mennonite Brethren was $40,500. If the church wished to reserve and remove the improvements on the land, $2,305 would be deducted from the total.[13] Apparently stunned by what was seen as a paltry offer, the mission board took two months to prepare a counterproposal. If officials in the Corps of Engineers thought they could easily take advantage of a group of unsophisticated Mennonite farmers and preachers, they soon found out otherwise.

On September 17 Janzen responded to the government's offer with a detailed breakdown and explanation of the estimated costs entailed in replacing their facilities and meeting the building codes of the state. The sixteen lots for a church and relocated buildings in Indiahoma cost $3,200. A modest cement-brick structure with a basement, large enough to replace three buildings used at Post Oak, would cost $54,288. Janzen pointed out that no amount of money could compensate for the "spiritual, cultural, or emotional" loss of "dear old Post Oak Mission, which since 1894 has cost labor, sweat, tears, life, and financial sacrifice on the part of God's people." The cost and sacrifice had been willingly expended by the Mennonites for the benefit of the Comanche people "with no expense to the American taxpayer." He stated that the mission board, with faith in the government's integrity, had "hoped and prayed" they would receive sufficient funds to construct at least one building—a church for the Indians. The $40,500 offered to them was woefully inadequate to accomplish that objective. According to their own conservative estimates, the total cost of the church project, including the land, would come to some $57,000. This figure, he emphasized, did not include the cost of furniture, sidewalks, gravel for the parking lot, landscaping, or his administrative expenses.

Janzen then sought diplomatically to shame the military into reconsideration. If the Department of Defense could not justify adequate reimbursement to the poor Indians who were being forced from their sacred religious grounds, the mission board had but one alternative. The board would have to go to the Mennonite constituency and ask them "to come to the assistance of our good Government" by contributing money and labor to make up the difference between the actual costs and what the army was willing to pay. He concluded with a request for an early response so they could proceed with plans and relieve the great anxiety of the Indian community.[14]

The army's Corps of Engineers kept the Post Oak Comanches and the Mennonite Brethren mission board dangling without a response for over three months, only announcing that their property must be vacated by July 1, 1957. In December 1956 the frustrated executive secretary addressed a letter to Senator Robert S. Kerr, with copies to Senator A. S. Monroney and Representative Toby Morris. He reviewed the eighteen-month history of his dealings with the Tulsa District of the Corps of Engineers and pointed out that he had received "no response of any kind" to his letter of September 17. He emphasized the bad predicament in which they had been placed. They could do nothing at Post Oak Mission or construct a new church at Indiahoma until they had a definite commitment from the army. Yet they were ordered to vacate Post Oak Mission within six months. He also mentioned the difficulty in obtaining structural steel and that prices were going up while they were kept waiting. He respectfully requested the senator's help in expediting the matter.[15]

Senator Kerr used his influence to get the army to act quickly and positively to the Mennonites' proposal. A. J. Becker, according to his son Dan, had been a friend of Senator Kerr. During the time Kerr was governor of Oklahoma, Sam Becker had been a member of his Bible class in Oklahoma City. Whether these factors influenced the senator is not known; however, within twelve days after Kerr contacted the Washington office of the Corps of Engineers, Janzen was notified that the mission board's offer to give up their property for $57,000 had been approved. Two days later the official documents were mailed to Janzen for execution. Senator Monroney's timely inquiries may also have helped to expedite the matter. Kerr wrote Janzen: "It is indeed gratifying to me that the Corps of Engineers have agreed to accept the offer of $57,000 which you made to them in this connection."[16]

The Post Oak congregation was not only greatly relieved but almost jubilant when Rev. Janzen personally delivered the news of the monetary settlement. They felt that finally they had won at least a partial victory over the army, which they saw as callous and insensitive to their plight.

The End of the Post Oak "Foreign" Mission Era

In concurrence with the Post Oak Indian leadership, the Board of Foreign Missions now decided to establish the mission complex, including the cemetery, on a twenty-five-acre plot of ground immediately west of the Indiahoma town limits. The new church was built on the property's southeast corner, facing a road that would later be named Post Oak Street. The cemetery was laid out to the west and southwest of the mission school. Joe and Anna Gomez's residence was moved to a lot inside the town. The old Kohfeld-Becker parsonage was purchased by Flora Niyah (Roach) and moved to a site half a mile west of Indiahoma. Henry Wiebe was the building contractor for the new church and J. W. Fast served as project foreman. A ground breaking service was held on February 7, 1957.[1]

The old Comanche "Jesus House," part of which dated back to 1896, was dismantled June 10 to 13, by a Mennonite crew of volunteers from Enid, Fairview, and Hillsboro, Kansas. The lumber that could be salvaged was trucked to Hillsboro for use in the construction of apartments for missionaries home on furlough.[2] Eleven other structures were either moved or dismantled. The mission complex had consisted of twelve buildings, all except one of frame construction. They were the church, a two-story eight-room parsonage, a small house for mission workers, a large two-story dining hall with living quarters above, an enclosed arbor, a two-unit dwelling for helpers and also used for destitute Indians at times, a home for the assistant missionary, a reinforced concrete building with a water tank on top, a house built by George Koweno for his use, a toolshed, poultry house, and a large barn. What A. J. Becker had feared and dreaded had now become reality: all the old landmarks were destroyed. For the older Comanches in particular, and the many friends of Post Oak, it was a sad time. In the eyes of Mennonite church leaders, this sixty-one-year old mission founded by a historic Peace Church became a forced sacrifice to the god of war.

Under the grave relocation contract, the government permitted heirs of the deceased, if any, to designate a reinterment site. As a result, initial plans to relocate all grave sites at the new Post Oak Cemetery at Indiahoma did not materialize. The contract provided the Mennonite Brethren Church $3,800 for the

The A.J. Becker's son Glenn stands on the site where the Post Oak "Jesus House" stood 1896 to 1957 (April, 1977). The expansion of Fort Sill forced the relocation of the mission. A concrete structure (not shown) reinforced with car body frames to support a huge water tank still stands despite battering from the army's firepower on a missile range. Rev. Becker had boasted that the structure would "last 1000 years."
Credit: Courtesy of Glenn Becker

purchase of land, construction of an arbor, landscaping, and other expenses associated with the cemetery relocation.[3]

A major controversy erupted over the question of where to move the graves of Quanah and Cynthia Ann Parker. Interested parties, much like circling vultures, sought for varying reasons, to seize this historic prize. A Texas group wanted the chief and his mother moved to a site in the northern part of the Lone Star State.[4] The city of Lawton offered to donate land along Highway 62 for a cemetery that would include Parker's grave and monument. They promised to turn it into a historic, sacred shrine.[5] Fort Sill worked hard to convince the Parker children that their father could best be honored by having his grave moved to the old army post cemetery.

A. E. Janzen notified the Cemetery Relocation Division, Corps of Engineers, that they had reserved a place in the new Post Oak Cemetery for the chief and his family. He explained that shortly before his death, Quanah had instructed he be buried on the grounds of Post Oak at the head of his people. The new cemetery had been carefully planned to assure "that the spirit of this trust" would be perpetuated in line with the chieftain's last orders. He further stated, "Should anyone succeed in moving the grave and monument to a place detached from the new Post Oak Cemetery where the Chief's Indians will lie buried, our Church will not seek to interfere, but the violation will rest on the conscience of the guilty person or persons breaking this trust."[6]

Ultimately six of the surviving Parker children were persuaded to choose the Fort Sill Army post cemetery for their father's reinterment. Quanah's oldest living daughter and To-pay disagreed; they wanted him buried with the other Comanches at Indiahoma. Then, when a Comanche tribal cemetery was authorized near Cache on Indian land, they sought to have Quanah's grave moved to that site. To-pay's main concern was that Quanah be buried with other members of the Comanche tribe, as he had requested.

To-pay claimed that as the sole surviving wife she had the right to choose the burial site. Through a lawyer she filed a petition with the U. S. Attorney requesting that Quanah's grave be moved to "West Cache Issue Cemetery."[7]   The Tulsa U. S. District Engineer was prepared to recognize her right to make the choice; however, this right was challenged by the six Parker children. The Parkers' lawyer answered To-pay's petition by claiming inaccurately that Quanah had "set aside To-pay in 1907 when statehood came to Oklahoma following an order from the United States Congress." It was alleged that Congress told the chief to pick one wife, whereupon he had selected To-nar-cy and lived with her until his death. (This scenario overlooked the fact that To-pay had been recognized as an heir in 1911 and shared in the estate, receiving the Star House as a home for her and her children by Quanah.) It was also charged that To-pay's advanced age and inability to speak, read, or write the English language rendered her incapable of making a proper decision. Perhaps the strongest argument was that under Comanche law or custom a widow lost her inheritance rights if she remarried. To-pay had been married for a period of time to a man named Jud Komah.[8]

The family dispute over the reburial of Quanah Parker was adjudicated in federal court by Judge Ross Rizley. The judge deplored the fact that "one as distinguished as the late Quanah Parker should have all this argument among his relatives about his burial place."[9] He heard testimony from Vernon Field, the attorney representing To-pay and Werahre Parker Tahmahkera, Quanah's daughter, and from the firm of Richardson and Cavanaugh, representing the other Parker siblings. Although To-pay and other respondents were in the court room, only the lawyers spoke. Field verified that To-pay had become Quanah's wife in 1894, bore him several children, all since deceased, and had lived with him until his death in 1911. As his only surviving wife, he claimed she should have the authority to carry out his expressed wish to be buried with his people. Werahre supported To-pay's position. The other Parker family members, through their attorney, claimed that To-pay had been "shed" by their father in 1907, had remarried, and under Oklahoma and Comanche law she had no standing in this matter.[10]

Judge Rizley issued his decision on July 12, 1957. He did not rule on the legality of Quanah's various marriages. He said: "The Court would be reluctant to say there was a valid common-law marriage between the respondent To-pay and the Indian chieftain," pointing out the Indian custom ran afoul of U.S. laws on plural marriages. On the other hand, he was "very reluctant to stigmatize the principals involved and judicially illegitimize the children that were born to To-pay and Quanah." Leaving that issue aside, he declared it was the court's duty to settle this dispute in a manner most likely to "give dignity to the ashes of this distinguished Indian chief and his illustrious mother." Furthermore, it was his belief that reburial should be at a site most likely to remain permanent "until the Angel Gabriel speaks." The judge concluded that the Fort Sill location would be "best for all concerned," and made that his official ruling.[11]

In the final analysis, Quanah Parker's own wish and request—to be buried with his Comanche people—apparently received no consideration from the federal judge. Whether his statement "until the Angel Gabriel speaks" would assure more permanence than the time-worn and oft-broken pledge "as long as the grass grows and the waters flow," remained to be seen.

Work on the removal of graves from Post Oak cemetery began on June 14, 1957. A brief, final memorial service was held that morning, bringing to a close the storied history of that historic Comanche and Mennonite Brethren site. Under the terms of the reinterment contract, each body was unearthed by use of hand tools only—no machinery was permitted—and the remains placed in a new, individual coffin for relocation. A representative of the Post Oak congregation was employed by the government as an on-site inspector to ensure that every transfer was handled in a respectful manner. James

Che-bah-tah was selected to serve in this capacity. Alton Wiebe was the Mennonite representative at the new Post Oak Cemetery site.

The Bureau of Indian Affair's authorization of a Kiowa, Comanche, and Apache cemetery one mile west of Cache resulted in the removal of 116 graves to that site. One body was reinterred in Deyo Mission cemetery. The remaining 640 graves, including the vaults of A. J. and Magdalena Becker, were moved to the Post Oak Cemetery at Indiahoma.[12] As a result of the prolonged litigation, Quanah Parker's grave was one of the last to be moved. The army and the court contended that his removal to Fort Sill would bring honor and dignity to the distinguished Comanche chief. But the inscription on the monument over the grave they caused to be taken from the picturesque Post Oak Cemetery was the supreme irony: "Resting here until day breaks and shadows fall and darkness disappears. . . ." These words sounded embarrassingly permanent.

The graves of Quanah and Cynthia Ann Parker prior to removal to the Old Post Cemetery, Fort Sill. Credit: The Center for Mennonite Brethren Studies, Fresno CA

The Becker Funeral Home of Lawton was asked to provide funeral assistance for a reburial ceremony for Quanah and Cynthia Ann Parker. Arranged by the Fort Sill army command, the service was held on August 9, 1957. It marked the third funeral for the chief, and the Becker family had been involved in all three. Missionary Becker conducted Quanah's funeral in 1911; four years later, after his grave was vandalized, he presided over the reburial. Now sons Peter and Glenn, who held a contract with Fort Sill, assisted in "final" rites, though the term could hardly be used with any assurance. The army wanted an impressive ceremony and ordered a large twenty gauge steel casket to house what remained of the respected "Last Chief of the Comanches."

Thousands of people attended the event at Fort Sill, held on a site that came to be called Chiefs Knoll. A military escort was dispatched to Cache to bring To-pay to the service, but she refused to go. Quanah's daughter, Werahre, also chose not to attend. To-pay would remain in virtual seclusion until her death six years later.

Parker family members attending the ceremony included Baldwin Parker, Neda Birdsong, Wanda Page, Alice Purdy, Tom Parker, and Len Parker. Although they were involved in the litigation that resulted in bringing the grave to Fort Sill, all had opposed the army takeover of their father's allotment and the Post Oak Cemetery. A reporter noted that there were tears in the eyes of seventy-one-year old Baldwin Parker as he sat quietly at the service. The trauma of the Parker grave removal was reflected in the penned observations of Herwanna Becker Barnard. She wrote: "Even the dead do not rest. Topai, last survivor of the seven wives of Quanah Parker, says, 'Where now? Sometimes I wake up crying at night. Indians cry, too.'"[13]

Relocation to Indiahoma ushered in a new era for the Post Oak Mission congregation. Traumatic though it was, the removal experience had strengthened the Indian church. Members were called upon to make major decisions affecting their future and the concept and necessity of functioning as a corporate body became more real to them. They gained confidence in their ability to assume the responsibilities soon to be placed upon them as an independent church congregation.[14] There had been problems and frustrations to overcome: frequent changes in the white Mennonite leadership during the 1950s, some personality clashes, confusion and uncertainties about the future, and difficulties in reaching consensus.

But the core of Indian leadership had remained steadfast. A. E. Janzen provided a stabilizing influence during this critical period. As the mission board's executive secretary and treasurer since 1945, he was an authority figure the Indians had come to trust. He made many trips to Post Oak from his office in Hillsboro, Kansas. He kept the congregation informed, listened to their concerns, discussed options, and gave guidance. Perhaps most importantly, the Indians sensed he was deeply concerned about their welfare and respected their views.

Prompted by Janzen and J. B. Toews, the Board of Foreign Missions now took official steps to change the status of the Post Oak congregation to a self-administering and self-supporting church. Some Comanche members had been ready for this action years earlier; one veteran deacon left the fellowship because he believed his talents were not appreciated or utilized. Others were hesitant to endorse this change. Fifteen years earlier when H. W. Lohrenz had called for the indigenization of foreign missions, Becker had given his support. Many overseas missionaries had balked at the proposed changes. In his last years at Post Oak, Becker's reports often mentioned the strong Indian leadership that had emerged. But in 1956 when missionary Dan Petker informed Jim Che-bah-tah, Herman Asenap, and Pete Coffee that they were going to start leading the services and presiding over meetings, they objected. "We can't do it," they said. Nevertheless, with Petker's guidance and encouragement, they began to assume those responsibilities.[15] A joke circulating among the young people revealed their view of the missionary-Indian youth relationship. "We won't be able to have any more wiener roasts," they said, "without the whites telling us whether to stick our wieners into the fire from the east side or from the west side." The board also decided to end its financial support for the parochial school, knowing that would force its closure since the Indians could not finance its operation.

Janzen used the occasion of the dedication of the new church sanctuary and cemetery grounds, March 23, 1958, to discuss with the church council the proposed new relationship. According to Walter Friesen, the last missionary to serve at Post Oak, the council gave a "cooperative response . . . showing a willingness to adjust to the new program and assume the new responsibilities." However, the announcement that the school would be closed as early as May 1958 was apparently a surprise and disappointment. The congregation wished to see the school continue. Rising costs and low attendance—forty-five in each of the last two years—apparently doomed the school in the eyes of the mission board.[16] Under the board's plan, the mission would on January 1, 1959 be temporarily placed under jurisdiction of the Board of Home Missions of the Southern District Conference. Approximately a year later the congregation would be admitted to the Southern District of Mennonite Brethren churches as an autonomous church.

Although the new sanctuary was not formally dedicated until March 1958, services had been held in the basement since July of the previous year. The first service in the sanctuary was held December 22, 1957 using temporary seating. On Christmas Eve, 225 people crowded into the church for the traditional yuletide service and exchange of gifts. The large turnout was a positive sign that loyalty to Post Oak and its traditions remained strong.[17]

D. J. Gerbrandt believed it was a mistake to close the Indian school, noting that many leaders in the Post Oak church received their early training there. A number of graduates went on to successful careers in a variety of occupations and professions. Several obtained advanced degrees in education. Dr. Jacquetta Parker McClung, great-granddaughter of Quanah Parker, stated that her career in higher education was made possible because as a young girl she had learned the joy and discipline of study at Post Oak Mission School.[18] The following served as teachers or staff assistants at the school during its brief history: Ruth Wiens, Dorothy Kopper, Martha Kroeker, Elizabeth Sawatzky, Henry Krahn, Raymond Reimer, Max Pahcheka, Milton Friesen, Alton Wiebe, Ruby Siebert, D. J. Gerbrandt, Dan Petker, Eldon and Laura Boese, Ray Vogt, Leo Heinze, and Walter Friesen.

The following list shows the church officers of the Post Oak Mission Church in 1958: Mooney Che-bah- tah, Sunday school superintendent; James Che-bah-tah, assistant Sunday school superintendent; Roxie Plumlee, choir director; Pete Coffee, Roxie Plumlee, Grace Hoahwah, congregational song leaders; Flora Roach, Grace Hoahwah, Pete Coffee, Herman Asenap, serving committee; Roxie Plumlee, Virgie Kassanavoid, Billy Joe Bigbow, Christian endeavor committee; Coreen Che-bah-tah, Virgie Kassanavoid, Carleton Hoahwah, Ann Koppaddy, young peoples committee.[19]

In 1959 the mission church was incorporated as the Post Oak Mennonite Brethren Church, thus assuming an equal and independent status in the denomination. There were forty-eight charter members.[20] Although several more names were soon added to the rolls, the figures reveal a significant decline in membership compared to earlier years. Walter Friesen attributed the lower number to "the passing away of the older Indian people and the moving away of the younger ones." There had been a sizeable decrease in the Indian population in the area since World War II. Church rolls during the last years of the mission period showed a membership of 170, but seventy of those listed no longer resided in the area. Fifty to seventy-five Indians generally attended Sunday worship services at the new Post Oak church. If the church was to survive and grow, according to Friesen, it would have to reach out to the white population. He noted that the younger generation, having had close contact with the white population in public schools and in the community, were "acculturated to the American ways." It was his view that assimilation had progressed to the degree that Indians "feel one with the whites and the whites with them." This assimilation, and the change in status from mission to church, made it possible and desirable, he believed, to have an integrated Indian and white congregation. Although Friesen could urge the Indiahoma church to pursue this course, those kinds of decisions were now the responsibility of the Indian congregation itself.[21]

The Legacy

As their first and best-known mission field, Post Oak stimulated a growing interest among Mennonite Brethren to expand the church's mission beyond its own borders. Mission board members and other church leaders frequently visited the Comanche mission and reported on its progress. The *Zionsbote*, published for a number of years at Medford, Oklahoma, regularly carried news and reports on the mission program and promoted support for missions. Many individuals from congregations throughout the United States and Canada gave money designated for the Indian work. Sunday schools, sewing circles, and Christian endeavors sent money and material goods. It was easy to recruit volunteers to donate time and labor for projects on the mission compound. The enthusiasm for the mission program reflected a growing zeal to "go into all the world and preach the gospel." Between 1899 and 1943, new Mennonite Brethren mission fields were opened in India, China, and Africa. Following World War II, mission work expanded into six more countries, with a total of 206 new missionaries commissioned for foreign service between 1945 and 1960.[1] The vote to establish Post Oak Mission in 1895 was an important, tangible step committing the Mennonite Brethren to become a missionary church in deed, not only in rhetoric.

The history of Post Oak Mission is in a real sense the history of Magdalena and Abraham J. Becker. They rescued the fledgling mission station from almost certain closure in 1907, and shaped it into a viable enterprise that had a significant impact on thousands of Comanches in southwestern Oklahoma. For thirty-seven years the two worked as partners, complementing each other's talents and diminishing individual shortcomings. In the traditional Mennonite Brethren view, Rev. Becker was the "called" and, therefore, the paid missionary, while Magdalena was the helpmate who assisted her husband in "his" work. Rev. Becker did not hold to this view, and the mission board soon recognized that in the Beckers they did not have a missionary and wife—they had a team with a single-minded purpose to missionize the Indians.

The key member of this team was Magdalena Becker. The personal relationships she developed with tribal women opened the door to a broader ministry at Post Oak. Initially, women came to the mission to take advantage of the services offered by the field matron.

Soon, an increasing number began to attend the religious services, usually bringing their children and husbands with them. She was also a pillar of strength and the driving force in the religious programming at the mission. Magdalena Becker's leadership, commitment, and talents were critical to the development of Post Oak into a station recognized for its concern for the spiritual and physical welfare of the Indian community. In combination with her husband's activities—an extensive Indian visitation program, caring for their poor, sick, and bereaved, burying their dead, development and care of the physical plant, and faithfully preaching and teaching the gospel of salvation—the couple had a multi-faceted and beneficent ministry.

As German Mennonites from Russia who were themselves experiencing Americanization pressures, the Beckers had some understanding of what the Indians were going through. Both Mennonites and Comanches had to adopt a new language, new customs, and identify with new cultural expectations. That Mennonites who were strongly resisting assimilation, at least of certain kinds, would be aiding the assimilation process of Native Americans was ironic. Actually, the Beckers did not promote all aspects of the government's civilization program. In their version of that program they sought to induce the Comanches to accept Christianity, get educated, adopt the Mennonite work ethic, and assume the white methods and standards in the domestic arts. Except for his personal preference for the peyote religion, these were the same "civilizing" elements that had been promoted by the progressive chief Quanah Parker. When Comanches became Christians, the Beckers expected them to give up their "worldly habits," but they never insisted they give up all their Indian ways.

Rev. Becker's missionary service spanned over five decades. After his wife's death in 1938, he served three more years at Post Oak. Thereafter, as long as his health permitted, he assisted at Lawton View and filled in at Post Oak as needed. Although Becker's direct involvement at the Indian mission became less frequent in his latter years, he continued to exert influence through his contacts with the mission board and his many Indian friends.

There were many changes that affected the Comanche people of Oklahoma during the Beckers' long period of service. When the couple arrived on the reservation at the turn of the century, the Comanches were a traditionally nomadic people still trying to adjust to a sedentary way of life and a forced acculturation program. Over half the fourteen hundred tribal members on the reserve still lived in tepees or tents. Their necessities of life were provided by the Indian

Office, later called the Bureau of Indian Affairs, through disbursements from Indian funds held in trust by the government. Their economic outlook was bleak. Their land base was rapidly eroding and the viability of agriculture limited by geography and climate. Government policy was creating a cycle of dependency. Diseases were rampant and the death rate was high. Few spoke English; without interpreters the Beckers had no ministry.

When A. J. Becker moved from the Post Oak compound early in 1941, all of the Comanches, approximately two thousand by then, lived in houses rather than tents; but many had only a small fraction left of their original allotted land on which to reside. Lacking land and work skills, large numbers were still dependent on the government for survival. There was considerable poverty. Most Post Oak Christians at that time were too poor to own an automobile, or if they owned one, did not have the money to keep it in repair. In earlier days they had come to the mission in horse-drawn wagons; by the 1940s they had to be bused in. Only a handful of Comanches remained who could not understand Becker's English sermons, and the young people were rapidly losing use of the tribal language. Federal Indian policy had stripped the Comanches of virtually all their land and much of the basis of their culture. According to a leading historian of Indian affairs, most Comanches were impoverished by the system and had developed "a painful dependence" on the Indian Bureau. "Resentful of the control exercised by the government over even the smallest details of their lives, yet believing that only by continued association with it could they maintain their status as Comanches, they found themselves in the dilemma that still confronts them today."[2]

Many Indians saw their lives altered dramatically during World War II. A large number left Comanche County to take wartime jobs or enter the military. Forrest Kassanavoid from the Indiahoma community gained acclaim as a member of a unit of Indian code talkers in the European theater of war. In the postwar era, as job opportunites declined in rural Oklahoma, many veterans and their families migrated to the urban areas, where they faced an uncertain future.

Despite many problems, a growing number of Comanches were adapting successfully to the majority culture and the American capitalistic system, even while trying to maintain their Indian identity. A 1953 survey of Indians comprising the Post Oak Mission family produced these findings: eleven were engaged in skilled labor; fifteen in common labor; six farmed; five were public school teachers; four did clerical work; one was a preacher; twenty-one had other steady employment; four served in the armed forces; three attended college; and four attended Corn Bible Academy. A "large number" of others worked at seasonable jobs such as picking cotton, gathering pecans, or other harvest activity. The study identified the Post Oak Mission family as "less than 200 people, including old people and little children."[3]

Christian missionaries had made an impact over the years. The Oklahoma Indian Baptist Association alone reported over five thousand baptisms in Indian churches between 1897 and 1953. There is no doubt that Magdalena Becker's work as field matron-missionary significantly improved the health and general lot of Quanah Parker's Quahada band. As one Comanche homemaker observed, the skills taught by Mrs. Becker were still helpful many years later "as [they were] passed down from generation to generation."[4] The Beckers' ministry was not strictly confined to a narrow religious realm; it was also geared to address the social and economic problems confronting the Indians. They helped many to adapt more successfully to the twentieth-century realities of life facing a people living in two worlds. The Beckers had left a tradition-bound, semi-isolated Mennonite community to live and work in an "English" and Indian world. Although their situation was not completely analogous to the Indian experience, they could, perhaps better than many, appreciate the difficulties confronting a people seeking to come to terms with a strange new world.

Official congregational records on Post Oak Mission are scarce. Fortunately, Rev. Becker periodically reported on the number of converts added to the church. Two years before his retirement from Post Oak he wrote that he had baptized 425 individuals, including eighty-five Mexicans and seventeen whites. Three to five more converts were added in his last year at the mission. (E. C. Deyo reported about the same number of baptisms during his tenure at the American Baptist Comanche Mission). Becker also stated that he buried over six hundred people in Post Oak Cemetery and built approximately three hundred coffins. Each year between 1907 and 1941 new converts were added to the Post Oak Mission rolls. New members were regularly enrolled during the missionary tenure of each of Becker's successors. In the mid-1950s a study of the eight remaining Baptist missions in the Oklahoma Indian Baptist Association reported they were all "very weak" with small attendance.[5] Post Oak Mission, on the other hand, exhibited sufficient strength and vitality to begin steps leading to a self-sustaining church.

Despite coming from a rather ingrown and reclusive German-Russian background, the Beckers developed a commendable sensitivity toward cultural differences. Male converts were baptized and not prevented from being active church workers even if they wore their hair in long braids. Pahcheka, frequently used as an interpreter, "Old Man" Beaver, Nah-wooksy, and Oscar Yellow Wolf were among the church members who never gave up their traditional Indian hairstyle. Becker approved the ordination as deacon of an Indian who had previously practiced polygamy. When another deacon, a respected leader in the church, remorsefully confessed to a secret sexual encounter away from the community, Becker accepted his repentance as sincere and was willing to forgive and forget. The Board of Foreign Missions, apprised of the situation by the deacon himself, felt otherwise. Speaking for the board, H. W. Lohrenz insisted the offender confess his sin before the entire congregation and be removed from his office. The board's ruling caused Becker considerable anguish. He argued that requiring the man to go public would be very divisive and needlessly set back the mission work. Since there was agreement that the deacon had sincerely repented, he believed it appropriate that knowledge of his transgression be limited to the missionaries and the board. Becker apparently won out in the end because the man continued to serve as deacon.

Although non-judgmental on most cultural differences, Becker held his Indians to high Mennonite Brethren church standards. They had to give up drinking, dancing, card playing, and other worldly amusements before they could be baptized. Anyone who smoked or played pool was not allowed to hold church office, although smokers were not automatically excommunicated as was the case in white Mennonite Brethren churches. Other pietistic strictures existed. The wife of a later missionary sought to dissuade Indian girls from the "sin" of wearing slacks. The Beckers remained adamantly opposed to the use of peyote for any alleged purpose, whether related to health or religion. And they worked diligently to instill the work ethic in the hearts and minds of the Native Americans, an endeavor for which they claimed a modest degree of success.

The distinguishing characteristic of the Beckers' missionary service was their identification with the Comanche people. Herman Asenap expressed the Indian perspective well: "They became one of us." According to John B. Toews, longtime member of the Board of

Foreign Missions, the Mennonite Brethren "style of operation" in foreign missions for over fifty years "bore the flavor of the colonial system of the 18th and 19th centuries. It was a ministry to a people with initiative and decisions lodged with the mission staff. The national Christians, helpers to the missionaries, followed assignments without the privilege of creative leadership." Programs were devised and controlled by the local missionary. Missionaries were sent out to save the "heathen" and report back to the churches.[6] But in evaluating the missionary careers of A. J. and Magdalena Becker, Toews wrote the following: "In recalling the ministry of the Beckers, there emerges one very inclusive image—their identification with the people to whom next to God, they had given their lives. . . . The Indians were their people and their love and ministry reflected that quality." Unlike Mennonite Brethren missionaries generally, he stated, the Beckers practiced "a ministry with a people rather than to a people."[7]

The Beckers were not totally free of the colonial mind-set. Rather than teaching and nurturing the native church to more effectively evangelize and become responsible for its own activities, they probably concentrated too much on "soul winning" meetings conducted by visiting white evangelists. As "father" and "mother" they found it difficult to turn their Indian "children" loose from their supervision—in the church or community. At times supervision was needed to protect the tribespeople from their rapacious non-Indian neighbors. But it was also exercised to undermine cultural traditions that Mennonites considered "worldly" or a waste of time. More so than the Beckers, some of their successors tended to believe they knew what was best for the Indians and made decisions affecting the church without their consultation.

Walter Gomez observed that it was the Beckers' "deep love for the Indians and Mexicans" that won them acceptance and made them so effective and appreciated. "They were always ready to put others first before themselves. . . they had no known enemies." Gomez noted that he had tried to convince Rev. Becker his preaching would be "more effective" if he became as fluent as Mrs. Becker and Anna Gomez in the Comanche language.[8] Dorothy Lorentino and Anona Birdsong Dean, granddaughters of Quanah Parker, developed a deep appreciation for the Beckers. Lorentino recalled, "They did everything for the Indians, from delivering babies to making coffins. They taught us how to cook, can, and sew. The Beckers stayed with families when they lost loved ones. They were like parents to the Indians." Dean approvingly noted that the Becker boys, much like their native friends, "would wail and carry on when an Indian died." The two women had other fond recollections: "They lived and died with us. They're buried in our cemetery." "They gave us religion and taught us how to live." "They were very gentle people." "They gave us a foresight to education, morals, ideals." And, "They are still an influence in our lives."[9] Their long involvement in church, community, and agency affairs made the Beckers well known in the area. Many referred to Post Oak Mission as the "Becker Mission." Today a street in Indiahoma bears the Becker name.

In one of his early reports from the field, A. J. Becker wrote, "Sometimes we talked too much, and at other times too little, but too often, we did not love enough."[10]   Nevertheless, his hundreds of reports and letters to the mission board and church publications contain many expressions of love and concern for the Post Oak Indians. Rev. and Mrs. Becker referred to the Comanches as "my Indians," or "our Indians." Rarely can one find—and then mainly in the earlier reports—a tone of condescension or condemnation. Racial prejudice is never evident. In the context of the times, and in comparison to many other missionary accounts, such sensitivity and lack of bias toward racial minorities was unusual. Mennonite Brethren, and other religionists, were not immune to anti-Indian, anti-black, and anti-Mexican attitudes and practices during this period of history. One Mennonite Brethren evangelist was cautioned by a church member not to go preach to the Comanches. "In the end they might be converted, and what shall we do then?" This person was apparently worried the Indians might want to move to his community and get involved in the social and religious life of his church.[11]

The Beckers also identified with the poor whites and the Mexican people, living in the shantytown section called Lawton View. A. J. Becker started the Mexican ministry in the Mennonite Brethren Conference as an outreach of Post Oak Mission. Anna Gomez, Felix Koweno, and other Post Oak members helped sustain the program until it became a separate mission in Lawton. Rev. Becker almost single-handedly rallied the conference to support a ministry to the poor of this land, not just to those overseas. With his death, and without his leadership, the Lawton View program languished and soon faded from the attention of the Mennonite Brethren constituency.[12]

Rev. Becker was not a deep theologian or a particularly polished preacher. He was humble, unsophisticated, down-to-earth. Rhoda Asenap Tate recalled Becker as a kindly man, "in his wrinkled suit, coat pockets stuffed with candy and treats for us young children; such love you will never experience again from anyone."[13] As with many recent immigrants, Becker's English spelling was poor; his letters abound with grammatical and typographical errors. In his administrative work, Becker collaborated closely with three executive secretaries of the Board of Foreign Missions. There is comparatively little correspondence in the board's files covering the years that N. N. Hiebert served in that position. The educated, well-spoken, and always grammatically correct H. W. Lohrenz developed a genuine affection and respect for the Beckers. Rev. Becker leaned on him for counsel on deeply personal matters and confided in him more than anyone else outside his own family. He even asked him for a list of potential marriage partners after the death of Magdalena. Lohrenz, with great reluctance and a stipulation of strict confidentiality, complied. However, Becker's second wife did not come from this list. Becker and A. E. Janzen also developed a good working relationship and mutual respect. Janzen leaned heavily on the advice of the veteran missionary. Although possessed of great patience, faith, and a sense of humor, the Beckers frequently confessed that their work was difficult, and caused them many tears. Unlike prevailing missionary practice, their reports were not just glowing accounts of success without the hint of failure or setbacks. Still they remained steadfast and undaunted.

The Beckers' first baptized convert, Sam Mo-wat, known as No Hand, outlived A. J. Becker by eleven months. Aged ninety when he died, his life began in a hunting and gathering culture, and ended in a hospital with the latest medical technology. He was a loyal member of Post Oak Mission for forty years. Her-wa-nee ("Dawn of Day") preceded Becker in death by nine days. Mary (Wi-e-puh) Koweno, another one of the "Founding Seven," died on October 31, 1954 at age 90. Herman Asenap, the faithful interpreter and respected elder, died in 1960. The longest survivor of the early converts was "Mattie" Maddische. Baptized in 1917, she was believed to be one hundred and ten years old when she died on September 15, 1986. The Comanche tribe named a new housing development, the "Maddische Estates," in her honor. Maddische was the mother of Lizzie Pahcheka, still active in the church, and Perry Heath, now deceased.[14] The resilient, tenacious To-pay finally succumbed to death November 19, 1963. Although ill and confined to a wheelchair in her latter years, she continued to worship regularly at the old Post Oak "Jesus House." Despite her frail health, she was described as "always a jolly person . . . and highly respected."[15] Records showed To-pay to be ninety-three at death, but she had claimed to be more than 100 years old.

Other Post Oak pioneers also passed from the scene. "Annie" and Joe Gomez died in 1971 and 1980 respectively, and were buried at the new Post Oak Cemetery. This humble, unpretentious couple made a positive and long-lasting impact on many hundreds of Indian and Mexican families in southwestern Oklahoma. During her many years of service Anna Gomez had experienced close brushes with death in several car accidents, a flash flood, and a house fire.[16] She is another example of the important role women played in the history of Post Oak Mission. Becker's wife Katharina, (Tina) who returned to Canada after his death, died on October 15, 1956.

The missionaries who served at Post Oak in the post-Becker era— John Dick, Clarence Fast, J. J. Wiebe, D. J. Gerbrandt, Herman Neufeld, Dan Petker, Walter Friesen—served relatively brief terms. Wiebe, Petker, and Friesen were interim appointments. Linda and Dick Gerbrandt's ten-year stay (counting one year on furlough) was the longest. They provided a sense of stability and direction that was missing under the frequently changing, short-term administrators.

Although new converts continued to be added during this period, statistical information is incomplete. Without exception, the missionaries and their children, in retrospect, recalled the warm acceptance and embracing love they experienced at Post Oak. "I learned about God's inclusiveness while growing up at Post Oak," the daughter of one missionary couple testified.[17] This does not mean there was no friction or conflict. Some missionaries were insentive at times to Indian culture and revealed feelings of superiority, but the Comanches were reluctant to voice their inner feelings or concerns to the white leadership.

The foundation for an Indian Mennonite Brethren Church in Oklahoma was established between 1894 and 1907. The initial groundwork was laid by Henry Kohfeld; A. J. and Magdalena Becker put the mission on solid footing. The dream of an Indian church became a reality in 1907 with the baptism of the first converts. In 1959, after sixty-four years under the auspices of the Board of Foreign Missions, the opportunities and responsibilities of further Christian service were placed in the hands of the Native Americans at Indiahoma. Perhaps the best tangible evidence of the "success" of the Mennonite Brethren mission to the Indians—and the basic criterion by which it should be judged—is the existence in 1996 of a Post Oak Indian congregation where God is still worshipped and obeyed.[18]

Epilogue

In 1995 Post Oak Mennonite Brethren Church celebrated the centennial of the founding of Post Oak Mission. Six pastors have served the church since 1960: Paul Kliewer, 1960-61; Joe Lonetree, 1962-64; Cycil Adrian, 1965-75; John Heidebrecht, 1975-77 and 1980-81; Herbert Schroeder, 1982-93; and Wilfred Niedo, 1995 to present.

Joe Lonetree, a Winnebago, was the first Native American to pastor a Mennonite Brethren church. He received Bible training at Cook Christian Training School in Phoenix, Arizona. His wife is Anna Bigbow Lonetree, whose family has a long connection with Post Oak. Lonetree has also served as assistant pastor on several occasions and, along with his wife, continues to be active in the life of the congregation.

Wilfred Niedo is the first Comanche to pastor the congregation. His family roots go deep into the mission era of Post Oak. He and his wife Jewell were married at old Post Oak by Rev. Herman Neufeld. Niedo's previous experience includes a ministry on the Navaho reservation and pastoring a Nazarene church at Cache.

During the 1960s and 1970s the church experienced steady growth. The membership in 1966 was eighty-four; by 1974 it had reached a peak of one hundred twenty-two. A number of whites and several Hispanic families became members during this period. Thus people with new Mennonite Brethren names like Figueroa, Ulloa, McGee, Arterberry, and Rowlings joined with the Comanches to assist the Kliewers, Adrians, Heidebrechts, and Schroeders in a common ministry.

In the early 1980s a disagreement within the church resulted in the establishment of a separate congregation at nearby Cache. Known as the Pete Coffee Memorial Church, it now functions as an independent congregation not affiliated with the Mennonite Brethren denomination.

Since 1960 the links between the Post Oak church and the Mennonite Brethren Conference have not been as close as during the mission period, when Indians regularly attended conference-wide church gatherings. The fault may well lie with the failure of the denominational leadership to integrate peoples without an ethnic German background into the life of the conference. As far as can be determined, not one Indian from Post Oak has ever been selected to serve on a General Conference or District Conference committee, or to hold any church leadership position outside the local congregation. During the eleven-year pastorate of Herbert Schroeder, a graduate of the Mennonite Brethren Biblical Seminary, a greater effort was made to involve the congregation in the activities of the conference.

At the end of 1995 there were 139 names on the membership roll of the Post Oak Mennonite Brethren Church, with fifty-seven identified as "active" members.[1] Many of the family names of the early mission converts are still represented in the congregation: Asenap, Bigbow, Cable, Codopony, Hernasy, Hoahwah, Kassanavoid, Koweno, Niedo, Ni-yah (Roach), Pahcheka, Tenequer. Likewise the style of worship, Comanche songs, children reciting verses on the stage (but no candy), and the Magdalena Circle meetings, are reminiscent of the old Post Oak Mission days. Based on the author's personal observations, church members still revere their ethnic and religious heritage, and seem determined to maintain both as they enter a second century of service on the Oklahoma plains.

Endnotes

PREFACE

1. J. F. Harms, *Geschichte der Mennoniten Brüdergemeinde, 1860-1924* (Hillsboro, Kansas: Mennonite Brethren Publishing House, 1924); John H. Lohrenz, *The Mennonite Brethren Church* (Hillsboro, Kansas: Mennonite Brethren Publishing House, 1950); Mrs. H. T. Esau, *First Sixty Years of M. B. Missions* (Hillsboro, Kansas: Mennonite Brethren Publishing House, 1954).

2. Gerhard W. Peters, *The Growth of Foreign Missions in the Mennonite Brethren Church* (Hillsboro, Kansas: The Board of Foreign Missions, 1952); Peters, *Foundations of Mennonite Brethren Missions* (Hillsboro, Kansas: Kindred Press, 1984); John A. Toews, *A History of the Mennonite Brethren Church* (Hillsboro, Kansas: Mennonite Brethren Publishing House, 1975); J. B. Toews, *Pilgrimage of Faith: The Mennonite Brethren Church, 1860-1990* (Winnipeg, Manitoba: Kindred Press, 1993).

3. See especially Clyde A. Milner II and Floyd A. O'Neil, eds., *Churchmen and the Western Indians, 1820-1920* (Norman: University of Oklahoma Press, 1985), and Clara Sue Tidwell, *Choctaws and Missionaries in Mississippi, 1818-1918* (Norman: University of Oklahoma Press, 1995).

PROLOGUE

1. This account is based on A. J. Becker, interview with Sam Becker, December 25, 1948, Glenn Becker Collection, Lawton, Oklahoma. Biographical information is in Glenn Becker Collection. Although some accounts state Becker's trip to the reservation occurred in fall 1895, evidence from government records authorizing the building program shows it could not have been earlier than spring 1896. See Acting Indian Agent to Mennonite Brethren Church, April 20, 1896, Kiowa Agency, Letterpress Book, Vol. 50, 264, Microcopy KA24, Archives/Manuscripts Division, Oklahoma Historical Society, Oklahoma City.

CHAPTER 1

1. For the founding of the Mennonite Brethren Church in Russia and Jacob Becker's role in its establishment see Jacob P. Bekker, *Origin of the Mennonite Brethren Church*, trans. D. E. Pauls and A. E. Janzen (Hillsboro, Kansas: Mennonite Brethren Publishing House, 1973). On the creation of a conference and the early activities of the Mennonite Brethren Church in North America see John H. Lohrenz, *The Mennonite Brethren Church* (Hillsboro, Kansas: Mennonite Brethren Publishing House, 1950), 61-88. See also Mrs. H. T. Esau, *First Sixty Years of M. B. Missions* (Hillsboro, Kansas: Mennonite Brethren Publishing House, 1954), 26. The appointment of Kohfeld is found in Minutes of the General Conference of the Mennonite Brethren Church, 1894, translated and edited by R. C. Seibel, General Conference Records, Center for Mennonite Brethren Studies, Hillsboro, Kansas.

2. Henry Kohfeld, "Meine Erfahrungen von der Liebe und Treue Gottes," *Zionsbote*, July 10, 1929, 12.

3. Stanley P. Dyck, "The Halstead Indian Industrial School," *Mennonite Life* (June, 1987): 4-10.

4. Donald J. Berthrong, *The Cheyenne and Arapaho Ordeal* (Norman: University of Oklahoma Press, 1976), 141.

5. Kohfeld, "Meine Erfahrungen," 12.

6. *Ibid.*, July 17, 1929, 13-14; J. F. Harms, *Geschichte der Mennoniten Brüdergemeinde, 1860-1924* (Hillsboro, Kansas: Mennonite Brethren Publishing House, 1924), 286-287.

7. Kohfeld, "Meine Erfahrungen," July 17, 1929, 13-14.

8. For a description of Comanche religion and society and their early history see Ernest Wallace and E. Adamson Hoebel, *The Comanches: Lords of the South Plains* (Norman: University of Oklahoma Press), 1952. Also consult Rupert N. Richardson, *The Comanche Barrier to South Plains Settlement* (Glendale: Arthur H. Clark , 1933). The most recent study is Thomas W. Kavanagh, *Comanche Political History: An Ethnohistorical Perspective 1706-1875* (Lincoln: University of Nebraska Press, 1996).

9. For a good overview of the Comanche response to the encroachment of whites into their territory and the military operations against them see William H. Leckie, *The Military Conquest of the Southern Plains* (Norman: University of Oklahoma Press, 1963).

10. A general survey of the government's policies towards the American Indians is provided in S. Lyman Tyler, *A History of Indian Policy* (Washington, D. C.: United States Department of the Interior, 1973). See also Francis Paul Prucha, *American Indian Policy in the Formative Years* (Cambridge: Harvard University Press, 1962).

11. Leckie, *The Military Conquest of the Southern Plains*, 14-18.

12. Charles J. Kappler, *Indian Laws and Treaties*, II (Washington, D. C.: Government Printing Office, 1903-27, 887, 893).

13. *Ibid.*, 977-78, 983-89.

14. For the most thorough treatment of the Comanche reservation experience see William T. Hagan, *United States-Comanche Relations: The Reservation Years* 1976; reprint, (Norman: University of Oklahoma Press, 1990).

15. The information on Quanah Parker is based on William T. Hagan, *Quanah Parker, Comanche Chief* (Norman: University of Oklahoma Press, 1993).

CHAPTER 2

1. Henry Kohfeld, "Meine Erfahrungen, von der Liebe und Treue Gottes," *Zionsbote*, July 17, 1929, 14, and July 24, 1929, 14-15; A. J. Becker, "The Story of Post Oak," *Zionsbote*, November 28, 1945; Richard H. Harper, "The Missionary Work of the Reformed (Dutch) Church in America in Oklahoma," *Chronicles of Oklahoma*, Vol. XVIII, No. 4 (December, 1940): 347.

2. A. E. Janzen, *Foreign Missions* (Hillsboro, Kansas: Mennonite Brethren Church of North America, 1946), 7-8.

3. William T. Hagan, *Quanah Parker, Comanche Chief* (Norman: University of Oklahoma Press, 1993), 47.

4. Kohfeld, "Meine Erfahrungen," July 17, 1929, 14, and July 24, 1929, 14-15.

5. Henry Kohfeld to Frank Baldwin, Indian Agent, Anadarko, Oklahoma Territory, October 21, 1895, Kiowa Agency, Churches, Microcopy KA50, Archives/Manuscripts Division, Oklahoma Historical Society, Oklahoma City; Frank Baldwin to Henry Kohfeld, Hillsboro, Kansas, October 29, 1895, Kiowa Agency, Letterpress Book, Vol. 47, 358, Microcopy K23, Oklahoma Historical Society.

6. Minutes of the General Conference of the Mennonite Brethren Church, October 28-29, 1895, trans. and edited by R. C. Seibel, General Conference Records, Center for Mennonite Brethren Studies, Hillsboro, Kansas.   Some sources either state or infer that Kohfeld's search for a mission field in Oklahoma took place in 1894, following the General Conference meeting in October of that year. See J. F. Harms, *Geschichte der Mennoniten Brüdergemeinde, 1860-1924* (Hillsboro, Kansas: Mennonite Brethren Publishing House, 1924), 287, and Mrs. H. T. Esau, *First Sixty Years of M. B. Missions*, (Hillsboro, Kansas: Mennonite Brethren Publishing House, 1954), 26. The evidence clearly points to 1895 as the actual date that this occurred. The most compelling evidence is found in the school records of Marion

County, Kansas which show that in 1894 Kohfeld was employed as a teacher in District 11, Hillsboro, Kansas. The school term did not end until April, 1895. See Clerk's Record, School District No.11, Marion County, Kansas, Center for Mennonite Brethren Studies, Hillsboro, Kansas. Further evidence supporting the 1895 date is the above correspondence between Kohfeld and Baldwin in 1895 and this reference in a Baptist missions publication dated August 21, 1926: "When the Mennonite Brethren Mission Board sought a location in 1895, the Deyo home was opened to them . . . . Post Oak Mission was located through his assistance and that of Dr. Marrow [sic]." Quoted in Janzen, *Foreign Missions,* 8-9. Also, Kohfeld's interpreter on his visit to Quanah Parker was said to be a convert of the Dutch Reformed Mission near Lawton. This mission was not established until 1895. See C. Ross Hume, "Pioneer Missionary Enterprises of Kiowa, Comanche, and Wichita Indian Reservation," *Chronicles of Oklahoma,* XXXIX, No.1(Spring, 1951): 115. In his 1929 recollections of his first visit to the reservation, Kohfeld, unfortunately, does not give the date. However, he makes several references to having endured hardships brought on by the hot weather. October through December are not hot weather months in Oklahoma.

   7. In a 1948 interview, Becker contributed to the confusion when he said that he came to Post Oak in 1895 to help with the construction program. A. J. Becker, Interview with Sam Becker, December 25, 1948. However, in an account written by Magdalena Becker in the 1930s, she stated that her husband's first trip to the mission was "along in 1896." "Post Oak Mission and the Becker Family," *Washita County Enterprise,* November 27, 1974.

   8. Frank Baldwin to Mennonite Brethren Church, February 26, 1896, Kiowa Agency, Letterpress Book, Vol. 49, 369, Microcopy KA24.

   9. Baldwin to Commissioner of Indian Affairs, March 10, 1896, Kiowa Agency, Letterpress Book, Vol. 51, 18, Microcopy KA25.

   10. J. F. Harms to Charles Curtis, March 17, 1896, Enclosure, Curtis to Commissioner of Indian Affairs, March 20, 1896, Letters Received, Office of Indian Affairs, Special Case 143, Kiowa Agency (10842-1896), National Archives, Washington, D. C.

   11. Charles Curtis to Commissioner of Indian Affairs, March 20, 1896, *Ibid.*

   12. D. M. Browning to Baldwin, March 24, 1896, Kiowa Agency, Churches.

   13. Harms to Curtis, April 6, 1896, Enclosure, Curtis to Commissioner of Indian Affairs, April 9, 1896, Letters Received, Office of Indian Affairs, Special Case 143, Kiowa Agency (13403-1896), National Archives.

   14. Curtis to Commissioner of Indian Affairs, April 9, 1896, *Ibid.*

   15. D. M. Browning to Frank Baldwin, April 14, 1896, Kiowa Agency, Churches.

   16. Baldwin to Mennonite Brethern [sic] Church, April 20, 1896, Kiowa Agency, Letterpress Book, Vol. 50, 264, Microcopy KA24.

   17. Baldwin to Commissioner of Indian Affairs, April 30, 1896, Kiowa Agency, Letterpress Book, Vol. 51, 61, Microcopy KA25.

CHAPTER 3

   1. Henry Kohfeld, "Meine Erfahrungen von der Liebe und Treue Gottes," *Zionsbote,* July 24, 1929, 15; A. J. Becker, "Our Experience While I was a Missionary and My Wife a United States Field Matron," Post Oak Mission Records, Mennonite Brethren Board of Foreign Missions, Center for Mennonite Brethren Studies, Fresno, California.

   2. On the establishment of Mennonite communities and churches in frontier Oklahoma see Marvin E. Kroeker, "Die Stillen im Lande: Mennonites in the Oklahoma Land Rushes," *Chronicles of Oklahoma,* LXVII, No.1(Spring, 1989): 76-97.

   3. Kohfeld, "Meine Erfahrungen," July 24, 1929, 15. Again, Kohfeld did not give the dates when these events occurred.

   4. Minutes of the General Conference of the Mennonite Brethren Church, October 28-29, 1896, trans. and edited by R. C. Seibel, General Conference Records, Center for Mennonite Brethren Studies, Hillsboro, Kansas.

5. Mrs. H. T. Esau, *First Sixty Years of M. B. Missions* (Hillsboro, Kansas: Mennonite Brethren Publishing House, 1954), 30.

6. *Ibid.*, 51.

7. Kohfeld, "Meine Erfahrungen," 15.

8. Ibid., 16; Dick Banks, Interview, March 18, 1938, Indian-Pioneer Papers, Vol. 5,11-15, Archives/Manuscripts Division, Oklahoma Historical Society, Oklahoma City; Herwanna Becker Barnard, "Comanches Cry, Too," *Prairie Lore* (October, 1978), 79.

9. Kohfeld, "Meine Erfahrungen," 16.

10. *Ibid.*, 15-16.

11. Henry Kohfeld Jr., Personal interview, May 27, 1994.

12. Maria Regier to *Zionsbote*, January 24, 1900; Kohfeld to *Zionsbote*, February 15, 1900.

13. A. J. and Magdalena Becker to *Zionsbote*, May 24, 1933.

14. Kohfeld, "Meine Erfahrungen," August 7, 1929, 14. Mennonite ministers commonly attributed favorable events or developments to Divine intervention, and believed that miracles might come through mortals here on earth. When they used terms such as "God spoke to me," or "God told me," it was generally interpreted to mean that the person had been prompted by an "inner voice" rather than an audible one.

15. *Ibid.*, July 31, 1929, 14-15.

CHAPTER 4

1. Glenn Becker Collection, Lawton, Oklahoma.

2. A. J. Becker, Interview with Sam Becker, December 25, 1948, Glenn Becker Collection.

3. David Charles Peters, ed., *Kudrich oba Lustig: Edited Writings of David Cornelius Peters (1883-1975)*, 19-40, Unpublished manuscript, Center for Mennonite Brethren Studies, Hillsboro, Kansas.

4. William T. Hagan, *Quanah Parker, Comanche Chief* (Norman: University of Oklahoma Press, 1993), 62-72, 93-101.

5. Blue Clark, *Lone Wolf v Hitchcock: Treaty Rights and Indian Law at the End of the Nineteenth Century* (Lincoln: University of Nebraska Press, 1994), 1-182.

6. A. J. Becker to *Zionsbote*, July 2, 1902.

7. Peters, ed., *Kudrich oba Lustig*, 23-24.

8. Mary Alice Maddox in *Post Oak Mission Centennial* (Oklahoma City: Taylor Publishing Co., 1995), 5.

9. W. J. Becker, "The Comanche Indian and His Language," *Chronicles of Oklahoma*, XIV, No. 3 (September, 1936): 340.

10. Peters, ed., *Kudrich oba Lustig*, 26-27.

11. Clark, *Lone Wolf v Hitchcock*, 48.

12. Verhandlungen der 24. Bundeskonferenz der Mennoniten-Brüdergemeinde in Nordamerika, abgehalten 1902, General Conference Records, Center for Mennonite Brethren Studies, Hillsboro, Kansas, 266.

13. Mrs. A. J. Becker to James F. Randlett, U. S. Indian Agent, August 30, 1904, Kiowa Agency, Field Matron Reports, Archives/Manuscripts Division, Oklahoma Historical Society, Oklahoma City.

14. Anna Deyo to Randlett, September 16, 1904, Field Matron Reports.

15. Affirmation of Mrs. Magdalena Becker as Asst. Field Matron, Indian Bureau Appointment, December 15, 1904, Field Matron Reports.

16. Robert E. Berkhover, Jr., *Salvation and the Savage, An Analysis of Protestant Missions and the American Indian Response, 1787-1862* (Lexington: University of Kentucky Press, 1965), 6-15.

17. Rebecca Herring, "Their Work Was Never Done: Women Missionaries on the Kiowa-Comanche Reservation," *Chronicles of Oklahoma*, 64 (Spring, 1986): 76.

18. Becker, Annual Report, August 31, 1905, Field Matron Reports.

19. Becker, Monthly Report, January 31, 1906, Field Matron Reports.

20. Ernest Wallace and E. Adamson Hoebel, *The Comanches: Lords of the South Plains* (Norman: University of Oklahoma Press, 1952), 121-123.

21. Lizzie Pahcheka, Personal interview, August 6, 1995.

22. These names were taken from various reports, 1906 forward.

23. Glenn Becker, Personal interview, March 20, 1995.

24. Anna Deyo, Monthly Report, October 31, 1906, Field Matron Reports.

25. Becker, Annual Report, December 31, 1906, Field Matron Reports.

26. John H. Lohrenz, *The Mennonite Brethren Church* (Hillsboro, Kansas: Mennonite Brethren Publishing House, 1950), 89-90.

27. Verhandlungen der achtundzwanzigsten Bundeskonferenz der Mennoniten-Brüdergemeinde in Nordamerika, abgehalten 1906, 351.

28. Peters, ed., *Kudrich oba Lustig*, 24; A. J. Becker, Interview with Sam Becker, December 25, 1948.

29. J. F. Harms, *Zionsbote*, August 7, 1929.

30. Peters, ed., *Kudrich oba Lustig*, 26.

31. Henry Kohfeld, Jr., Personal interview, May 27, 1994.

32. James C. Juhnke, "General Conference Mennonite Missions to the American Indians in the Late Nineteenth Century," *Mennonite Quarterly Review* (April, 1980): 127.

33. John Preston Dane, "A History of Baptist Missions Among the Plains Indians of Oklahoma," (Ph.D diss., Central Baptist Theological Seminary, Kansas City, Kansas, 1955), 95.

CHAPTER 5

1. Magdalena Becker to Mrs. H. T. Esau, March 7, 1938, Post Oak Mission Records, Mennonite Brethren Board of Foreign Missions, Center for Mennonite Brethren Studies, Fresno, California.

2. A. J. Becker, Interview with Sam Becker, December 25, 1948, Glenn Becker Collection, Lawton, Oklahoma.

3. Magdalena Becker to Mrs. H. T. Esau, March 7, 1938, Post Oak Records, Board of Foreign Missions.

4. Sources do not agree on the details of the accidental injury to Mo-Wat. A fictionalized account of this event, written for children, is found in Margaret A. Epp, *No Hand Sam and Other Missionary Stories* (Hillsboro, Kansas: Mennonite Brethren Publishing House, 1959), 5-11. However, No Hand was not converted as a young boy, as told in this story.

5. *The Indian Messenger,* February, 1954; David Charles Peters, ed., *Kudrich oba Lustig: Edited Writings of David Cornelius Peters (1883-1975)*, 25, 27, Unpublished manuscript, Center for Mennonite Brethren Studies, Hillsboro, Kansas.

6. Peters, ed., *Kudrich oba Lustig*, 27.

7. Glenn Becker and Marjorie Gerbrandt Wiens, Personal interviews, November 11, 1995.

8. Herwanna Becker Barnard, "The Comanche and His Literature, with an Anthology of His Myths, Legends, Folktales, Oratory, Poetry, and Songs," (M.A. thesis, University of Oklahoma, 1941), 72, 269-270.

9. Ernest Wallace and E. Adamson Hoebel, *The Comanches: Lords of the South Plains* (Norman: University of Oklahoma Press, 1952), xi.

10. Arlene Asenap, "Herman Asenap," in *Comanche County History* (Dallas: Curtis Media Corporation, 1985), 192-193.

11. Donald J. Berthrong, *The American Indian: From Pacifism to Activism* (Saint Louis: Forum Press, 1973), 4.

12. Minutes of the General Conference of the Mennonite Brethren Church, 1915,

trans. and edited by R. C. Seibel, General Conference Records, Center for Mennonite Brethren Studies, Hillsboro, Kansas.

13. *Ibid.*,

14. Church Roll and Record Book, Post Oak Mennonite Brethren Church, Indiahoma, Oklahoma.

15. Marjorie Kelley, Personal interview, August 6, 1995.

16. Minutes of the General Conference, 1907, trans. and edited by R. C. Seibel.

17. William T. Hagan, *United States-Comanche Relations: The Reservation Years* 1976; reprint,(Norman: University of Oklahoma Press, 1990), 229-231.

18. A. J. Becker to H. W. Lohrenz, January 27, 1915, Post Oak Records, Board of Foreign Missions; Hagan, *United States-Comanche Relations*, 287; For a detailed account of the early food distribution program on the reservation consult Marvin E. Kroeker, *Great Plains Command: William B. Hazen in the Frontier West* (Norman: University of Oklahoma Press, 1976), 80-90.

19. Minutes of the General Conference, 1908, 1909, and 1912, trans. and edited by R. C. Seibel.

20. A. J. Becker to *Zionsbote*, April 20, 1910.

21. *Ibid.*

22. Becker to H. W. Lohrenz, June 7, 1911, Post Oak Records, Board of Foreign Missions.

23. *Ibid.*, January 27, 1915.

24. *Ibid.*, June 7, 1911; *Post Oak Mission Centennial* (Oklahoma City: Taylor Publishing Company, 1995), 15.

25. Becker to Lohrenz, July 27, 1910 and October 26, 1910, Post Oak Records, Board of Foreign Missions.

26. Glenn Becker, Personal interview, May 1, 1994.

27. Carleton Hoahwah, Personal interview, March 19, 1995. According to Hoahwah, his great-grandfather, Hoahway, of Spanish birth, was captured in Mexico at the age of eight.

28. A. J. Becker to *Zionsbote*, October 4, 1911.

29. Minutes of the General Conference, 1915, trans. and edited by R. C. Seibel; *Church Roll and Record Book*, Post Oak Mennonite Brethren Church, Indiahoma, Oklahoma.

30. Minutes of the General Conference, 1915, trans. and edited by R. C. Seibel.

31. Magdalena Becker, Annual Report, August 13, 1913, Kiowa Agency, Field Matron Reports, Archives/Manuscripts Division, Oklahoma Historical Society, Oklahoma City; Ophelia D. Vestal, "The Post Oak Mission Cemetery," Indian-Pioneer Papers, Vol. 97, 379, Archives/Manuscripts Division, Oklahoma Historical Society.

32. A. J. Becker, undated manuscript, Post Oak Records, Board of Foreign Missions.

33. Magdalena Becker, Annual Report, August 13, 1913; Quarterly Report, September 30, 1914, Field Matron Reports; Lisa Emmerich, "'To Respect and Love and Seek the Ways of White Women': Field Matrons, the Office of Indian Affairs, and Civilization Policy, 1890-1938," (Ph. D. diss., University of Maryland, 1987), 214.

34. A. J. Becker, "Our Experience While I Was A Missionary and My Wife A United States Field Matron," no date, Post Oak Records, Board of Foreign Missions.

35. Herwanna Becker Barnard, "Comanches Cry, Too," *Prairie Lore* (October, 1978), 80.

36. Becker to Ernest Stecker, Indian Agent, March 19, 1908, Field Matron Reports.

37. Anna Deyo, Monthly Report, May 31, 1908, Field Matron Reports.

38. Becker, Quarterly Report, December 31, 1910, Field Matron Reports.

39. *Survey of the Condition of Indians in the U. S.*, Hearings, Subcommittee of Indian Affairs, U. S. Sen., 71st Cong., 33rd Sess., November 17-22, 1930 (Washington D. C.: U. S. Printing Office, 1931), 72267.

40. A. J. Becker to *Zionsbote*, August 2, 1911.

CHAPTER 6

1. William T. Hagan, *Quanah Parker, Comanche Chief* (Norman: University of Oklahoma Press, 1993), 127.

2. *Ibid.*, 48.

3. *Lawton Constitution,* November 20, 1963.

4. Herbert Woesner, Personal interview, March 18, 1996.

5. Buster Parker, Comments at the centennial observance of Post Oak Mission, Indiahoma, Oklahoma, November 11, 1995.

6. Herbert Woesner, Personal interview, March 18, 1996.

7. Carleton Hoahwah, Comments at the centennial observance of Post Oak Mission, Indiahoma, Oklahoma, November 11, 1995.

8. Opal Hartsell Brown, "Russian Refugee—Missionary to the Indians," *Prairie Lore* (April, 1979): 227.

9. Hagan, *Quanah Parker*, 115-116.

10. A. J. Becker, "Our Experience While I Was a Missionary and My Wife a United States Field Matron," no date, Post Oak Mission Records, Mennonite Brethren Board of Foreign Missions, Center for Mennonite Brethren Studies, Fresno, California.

11. J. Evetts Haley, "The Last Great Chief," *The Shamrock* (Spring, 1957): 18.

12. A. J. Becker, Interview with Sam Becker, December 25, 1948, Glenn Becker Collection, Lawton, Oklahoma.

13. A. E. Janzen, *Foreign Missions* (Hillsboro, Kansas: Mennonite Brethren Church of North America, 1946), 37.

14. Magdalena Becker to *Zionsbote*, November 29, 1911.

15. Magdalena Becker, Monthly Report, December 31, 1910, Kiowa Agency, Field Matron Reports, Archives/Manuscripts Division, Oklahoma Historical Society, Oklahoma City, Oklahoma.

16. Daniel A. Becker, "Comanche Civilization, with History of Quanah Parker," *Chronicles of Oklahoma*, I, No. 3 (June, 1923): 247; Margaret Schmidt Hacker, *Cynthia Ann Parker: The Life and the Legend* (El Paso: Texas Western Press, 1990), 32, 35; Magdalena Becker to *Zionsbote*, November 29, 1911.

17. *Daily Oklahoman*, February 24, 1911; Glenn Becker, Personal interview, August 13, 1995; Daniel A. Becker, "Comanche Civilization," 248; Interview with Harry Stroud, January 5, 1938, Indian-Pioneer Papers, Vol. 87, 387-388, Archives/Manuscripts Division, Oklahoma Historical Society; Magdalena Becker Memorandum Book, February 23, 1911, Sam and Elsie Becker Collection, Oklahoma City, Oklahoma.

18. *Cache Register*, March 3, 1911; Magdalena Becker to *Zionsbote*, November 29, 1911.

19. *Ibid.*

20. Magdalena Becker to *Zionsbote*, November 29, 1911; A. J. Becker to *Zionsbote* June 7, 1911.

21. *Cache Register*, March 10, 1911.

22. Brown, "Russian Refugee," 228; Hagan, *Quanah Parker*, 124.

23. Herwanna Becker Barnard, "Comanches Cry, Too," *Prairie Lore* (October, 1978): 78.

CHAPTER 7

1. Ernest Stecker to Commissioner of Indian Affairs, December 23, 1914, Kiowa Agency, Field Matron Reports, Archives/Manuscripts Division, Oklahoma Historical Society, Oklahoma City.

2. Magdalena Becker, Annual Report, December 31, 1914, Field Matron Reports; Kiowa Agency to Becker, February 26, 1915, Field Matron Reports; Becker to E. Stecker, March 4, 1915, Field Matron Reports.

3. Minutes of the General Conference of the Mennonite Brethren Church, 1915, trans. and edited by R. C. Seibel, Center for Mennonite Brethren Studies, Hillsboro, Kansas.

4. *Ibid.*

5. Personal interview, Marjorie Koweno Kelley, November 11, 1995.

6. ElRoy Ratzlaff, *God's Call to Mexico: The Story of Rev. Walter Gomez, Founder of MMM* (Pharr, Texas: Mexican Mission Ministries, Inc., 1994), 1.

7. Arrell M. Gibson, *The American Indian: Prehistory to the Present* (Lexington, Mass: D. C. Heath and Company, 1980), 431-434; Margaret Connell Szasz, *Education and the American Indian* (Albuquerque: University of New Mexico Press, 1974), 8-15.

8. Magdalena Becker to *Zionsbote*, November 29, 1911.

9. Becker, Annual Report, August 13, 1913, Field Matron Reports.

10. Superintendent to Magdalena Becker, June 15, 1915, Field Matron Reports.

11. Marjorie Kelley in *Post Oak Mission Centennial* (Oklahoma City: Taylor Publishing Company, 1995), 15.

12. J. F. Harms, *Geschichte der Mennoniten Brüdergemeinde* (Hillsboro, Kansas: Mennonite Brethren Publishing House, 1924), 290.

13. A. J. and Magdalena Becker to Rev. Abr. Schellenberg, September 10, 1907, Post Oak Mission Records, Board of Foreign Missions, Center for Mennonite Brethren Studies, Fresno, California.

14. Dorothy Sunrise Lorentino, Comments made at the centennial observance of Post Oak Mission, November 10, 1995, Indiahoma, Oklahoma.

15. Becker, Annual Report, August 13, 1913, Field Matron Reports.

16. Magdalena Becker to *Zionsbote*, November 6, 1912.

17. A. J. Becker to *Zionsbote*, June 7, 1911.

18. *Ibid.*, November 8, 1916.

19. Glenn Becker, Personal interview, March 20, 1995.

20. A. J. Becker to *Zionsbote*, August 25, 1915.

21. *Ibid.*, October 6, 1915; November 6, 1912.

22. *Ibid.*, December 19, 1917.

23. *Ibid.*, November 8, 1916.

24. *Ibid.*

25. Minutes of the General Conference, 1919, trans. and edited by R. C. Seibel.

26. A. J. Becker to *Zionsbote*, October 30, 1918.

27. Magdalena Becker, Monthly Report, November 22, 1918, Field Matron Reports.

CHAPTER 8

1. A. J. Becker and Magdalena Becker to *Zionsbote*, November 8, 1916.

2. Magdalena Becker, Monthly Reports, October 21, 1916 and August 2, 1919, Kiowa Agency, Field Matron Reports, Archives/Manuscripts Division, Oklahoma Historical Society, Oklahoma City.

3. Magdalena Becker to *Zionsbote*, July 30, 1919.

4. Becker, Monthly Reports, January through December, 1918, Field Matron Reports.

5. One twentieth-century Comanche medicine woman unequivocally stated that a patient who did not believe in her power could not be healed by her. David E. Jones, *Sanapia: Comanche Medicine Woman* (Prospect Heights, Illinois: Waveland Press, Inc., 1984), 82. In respect to the element of faith or belief in the practice of Indian medicine in the Comanche tribe see also Ernest Wallace and Adamson Hoebel, *The Comanches: Lords of the South Plains* (Norman: University of Oklahoma Press, 1952), 159.

6. Becker, Monthly Report, February 28, 1919, Field Matron Reports.

7. Nora Parker to Louise Driscoll, June 18, 1919; Driscoll to Supt. C. V. Stinchecum, June 20, 1919; Stinchecum to Driscoll, July 22, 1919, Field Matron Reports.

8. David Charles Peters, ed., *Kudrich oba Lustig: Edited Writings of David Cornelius Peters*

(1883-1975), 28, Unpublished manuscript, Center for Mennonite Brethren Studies, Hillsboro, Kansas.

   9. Magdalena Becker, Report, July 10, 1920, Field Matron Reports.

   10. *Ibid.*, February 28, 1920.

   11. *Ibid.*, December 8, 1923.

   12. Minutes of the General Conference of the Mennonite Brethren Church, 1919, trans. and edited by R. C. Seibel, Center for Mennonite Brethren Studies, Hillsboro, Kansas.

   13. Magdalena Becker to C. V. Stinchecum, April 2, 1919, Field Matron Reports.

   14. L. M. Gensman to C. V. Stinchecum, July 19, 1919; Stinchecum to M. Becker, September 13, 1919; Becker to Stinchecum, September 19, 1919 and October 6, 1919, Field Matron Reports.

CHAPTER 9

   1. A. J. Becker to J. W. Wiens, October 1, 1923, Post Oak Mission Records, Board of Foreign Missions, Center for Mennonite Brethren Studies, Fresno, California.

   2. Becker to N. N. Hiebert, November 29, 1933, Post Oak Mission Records.

   3. Blue Clark, *Lone Wolf v Hitchcock: Treaty Rights & Indian Law at the End of the Nineteenth Century* (Lincoln: University of Nebraska Press, 1994), 95-96, 161.

   4. A. J. Becker to J. W. Wiens, October 1, 1923; A. J. Becker to N. N. Hiebert, November 29, 1933; Magdalena Becker to J. W. Wiens, October 16, 1930, Post Oak Mission Records.

   5. William T. Hagan, *United States-Comanche Relations: The Reservation Years* (1976: reprint, Norman: University of Oklahoma Press, 1990), 277.

   6. *Annual Report of the Board of Indian Commissioners, U. S. Department of the Interior, For the Year Ended June 30, 1932* (Washington D. C.: U. S. Government Printing Office, 1932), 31.

   7. Magdalena Becker, Reports for the years 1922-1924, Kiowa Agency, Field Matron Reports, Archives/Manuscripts Division, Oklahoma Historical Society, Oklahoma City; *Cache Register*, February 3, 1911.

   8. Mrs. H. T. Esau, *First Sixty Years of M. B. Missions* (Hillsboro, Kansas: Mennonite Brethren Publishing House, 1954), 44-45.

   9. H. W. Laugheim, Physician, to A. G. Wilson, August 12, 1924, Kiowa Agency, Employee Records, Archives/Manuscripts Division, Oklahoma Historical Society.

   10. Mary Alice Maddox, Personal interview, August 6, 1995.

   11. A. J. and Magdalena Becker to Board of Foreign Missions, October 15, 1928, Post Oak Mission Records.

   12. *Ibid.*

   13. Ernest Wallace and E. Adamson Hoebel, *The Comanches: Lords of the South Plains* (Norman: University of Oklahoma Press, 1952), 168, 177-178.

   14. Esau, *First Sixty Years of M. B. Missions*, 44.

   15. *Daily Oklahoman,* May 4, 1930.

   16. *Lawton Constitution,* May 5, 1930; *Lawton News Review,* May 8, 1930.

CHAPTER 10

   1. Lisa E. Emmerich, "'To Respect and Love and Seek the Ways of White Women': Field Matrons, the Office of Indian Affairs, and Civilization Policy, 1890-1938," Ph. D. dissertation, University of Maryland, 1987, 296, 304-310. Emmerich has provided one of the few comprehensive studies on the field matron program. She concluded that "Within the context of its intended goal, the civilization of Native American women, the program was a near-total failure. Some Indian women did exhibit signs of increasing acculturation, thanks to the field

matrons' efforts. They wore `citizens' dress, attempted to keep house in the manner of white women, varied their diets, and adopted some aspects of Victorian gender ideology. All too often, though, the field matrons' victories were superficial and fleeting. Substantive, enduring changes in the lives of Native American women alluded them. . . . The field matrons never succeeded in convincing Native American women that the way of life they promoted was preferable to traditional lifestyles." My research on Magdalena Becker would indicate that Emmerich's use of the word "never" is clearly an overstatement. On the positive side, Emmerich believed that their health work successfully improved the quality of many Indian lives and "kept the field matron program from complete failure." *Ibid.,*   317-318.   Rebecca Jane Herring, in her study of the government's assimilation programs on the Kiowa-Comanche Reservation, concluded that the field matrons were quite successful in teaching household arts, but that the main goal of assimilating the Indians into American society was not reached. Her study of field matrons extended only through 1906, too brief a period to properly evaluate the program.   Rebecca Jane Herring, "Failed Assimilation: Anglo Women on the Kiowa-Comanche Reservation, 1867-1906," M. A. thesis, Texas Tech University, 1983, 134-135.

2. *Survey of the Conditions of Indians in the US.* Hearings before a Subcommittee of Indian Affairs, United States Senate, 71st Cong., 3rd Session, November 17-22, 1930 (Washington, D. C.: U. S. Government Printing Office, 1931), 7267, 7424-7425.

3. *Ibid.,* 7270; A. J. Becker to J. W. Wiens, April 23, 1931, Post Oak Mission Records, Board of Foreign Missions, Center for Mennonite Brethren Studies, Fresno, California.

4. US Department of the Interior, *Annual Report of the Board of Indian Commissioners, 1932* (Washington, D. C.: U. S. Government Printing Office, 1932), 31-32; *Survey of Conditions of Indians in the United States,* 7268.

5. Unfortunately, the Department of the Interior on several occasions approved the destruction of over 7000 field matron reports and related items. Some of Becker's later reports apparently were among those destroyed. Emmerich, "'To Respect and Love and Seek the Ways of White Women,'" 310. A review of Becker's personal record books indicates that the number of Indians she served did not decline after 1924.

6. Magdalena Becker, Monthly Time Book, June 30, 1932, Sam and Elsie Becker Collection, Oklahoma City, Oklahoma

7. A. J. Becker to H. W. Lohrenz, July 29, 1936, Post Oak Mission Records.

8. *Ibid.,* February 27, 1937; March 29, 1937; H. W. Lohrenz to Becker, May 30, 1937, Post Oak Mission Records.

9. A. J. Becker to H. W. Lohrenz, August 23 and November 8, 1937, Post Oak Mission Records.

10. *Ibid.,* June 18, 1938 and June 28, 1938.

11. A. J. Becker, "Biography of Mrs. Magdalena Hergert Becker," *Christmas Greetings* (Board of Foreign Missions, December, 1942), 25-26, Post Oak Mission Records.

12. *Lawton Constitution,* July 11, 1938; Luetta Reimer, "Mother to the Comanches," in Katie Wiebe, ed., *Women Among the Brethren* (Hillsboro, Kansas: Board of Christian Literature of the General Conference of the Mennonite Brethren Church, 1979), 104.

13. A. J. Becker, "Biography of Mrs. Magdalena Hergert Becker," 26.

CHAPTER 11

1. A. J. Becker to H. W. Lohrenz, September 8, 1938; September 29, 1938; October 8, 1938; December 22, 1938; January 3, 1939; Lohrenz to Becker, December 26, 1938, Post Oak Mission Records, Board of Foreign Missions, Center for Mennonite Brethren Studies, Fresno, California.

2. Becker to Lohrenz, August 2, 1939, Post Oak Mission Records.

3. *Ibid.,* December 15, 1939; January 25, 1940.

4. Lohrenz to Becker, March 11, 1940 and July 29, 1940, Post Oak Mission Records.

5. Becker to Lohrenz, August 10, 1940, Post Oak Mission Records.

6. *Ibid.*, April 19, 1940 and May 22, 1940

7. *Ibid.*, January 3, 1941; January 30, 1941; February 29, 1941; undated letter, 1941.

8. *Ibid.*, April 3, 1941; June 1, 1941. One of the changes Dick sought to make was the manner in which Christmas was celebrated at the mission. He thought that the families should distribute their gifts at home. This proposal was not well-received and firmly rejected by the Indians.

9. Lohrenz to Becker, October 11, 1940, Post Oak Mission Records.

10. Becker to Lohrenz, March 1, 1941; August 21, 1943; December 29, 1943, Post Oak Mission Records.

11. *Ibid.*, November 25, 1941; December 2, 1941; Elsie Becker, Personal Interview, October 17, 1996.

12. Mrs. H. T. Esau, *First Sixty Years of M. B. Missions* (Hillsboro, Kansas: Mennonite Brethren Publishing House, 1954), 32-33.

13. This report circulated in Corn.

14. Esau, *First Sixty Years of M. B. Missions*, 41-42; Wilma Dick Wall, Comments made at the centennial observance of Post Oak Mission, Indiahoma, Oklahoma, November 12, 1995.

15. Minutes of Post Oak Business Committee, May 10 and May 24, 1942, Post Oak Mission Records.

16. A. E. Janzen, *Foreign Missions* (Hillsboro, Kansas: Mennonite Brethren Church of North America, 1946), 25-26.

17. Esau, *First Sixty Years of M. B. Missions*, 55; Janzen, *Foreign Missions*, 25-26.

18. Janzen, *Foreign Missions*, 27.

19. Becker to Lohrenz, February 3, 1944; March 4, 1944; August 31, 1944; February 1, 1945, Post Oak Mission Records; ElRoy Ratzlaff, *God's Call to Mexico: The Story of Rev. Walter Gomez, Founder of MMM* (Pharr, Texas: Mexican Mission Ministries, Inc., 1994), 3.

20. Becker to Janzen, July 12, 1946; Janzen to Becker, July 15, 1946, Post Oak Mission Records.

21. Becker to Janzen, November 14, 1946, Post Oak Mission Records.

22. *Ibid.*, August 6, 1947; October (no date), 1947.

23. *Ibid.*, August 6, 1947.

24. *Ibid.*, October (no date), 1947; Janzen to Becker, November 12, 1947, Post Oak Mission Records.

25. Becker to H. W. Lohrenz, February 1, 1945, Post Oak Mission Records.

26. Becker to Janzen, February 1, 1946, Post Oak Mission Records.

27. Don Parman, *Indians and the American West in the Twentieth Century* (Bloomington: Indiana University Press, 1994), 89-106.

28. Esau, *First Sixty Years of M. B. Missions*, 52-53.

29. Becker to Janzen, June 4, 1948, Post Oak Mission Records.

30. *Ibid.*

31. Janzen to Becker, June 16, 1948, Post Oak Mission Records.

32. Edith Kassanavoid Gordon, Personal interview, November 12, 1995; Dick J. Gerbrandt, Letter to author, October 10, 1995.

33. Minutes of Board of Foreign Missions, April 26, 1948, M. B. Mission/Services, Box 1, Center for Mennonite Brethren Studies, Fresno, California.

34. Ibid, June 22-23, 1949.

35. Dick J. Gerbrandt, Letter to author, October 10, 1995.

36. Dick J. Gerbrandt, Comments made at the centennial commemoration of Post Oak Mission, Indiahoma, Oklahoma, November 10, 1995.

CHAPTER 12

1. A. J. Becker to A. E. Janzen, January 8, 1948, Post Oak MissionRecords, Board of Foreign Missions, Center for Mennonite Brethren Studies, Fresno, California.
2. Becker to P. R. Lange, June 4, 1948, Post Oak Mission Records.
3. Glenn Becker to A. E. Janzen, August 25, 1948, Post Oak Mission Records.
4. A. E. Janzen to Becker, September 20, 1948; H. W. Lohrenz to Becker, February 28, 1949; Becker to Janzen, July 19, 1949, Post Oak Mission Records.
5. Becker to Janzen, December 22, 1949, Post Oak Mission Records
6. *Ibid.*, October 29, 1952.
7. Becker to Mr. Fayne and Neda Birdsong, October 23, 1952; Becker to Janzen, October 29, 1952, Post Oak Mission Records.
8. Becker to Janzen, Undated letter, Post Oak Mission Records.
9. Janzen to Becker, October 31, 1952, Post Oak Mission Records.
10. Gen. Miles Reber to Robert S. Kerr, undated letter, Robert S. Kerr Papers, Topical Box 14, Carl Albert Congressional Research and Studies Center, University of Oklahoma, Norman.
11. Glenn Becker, Personal interview, November 11, 1995.
12. *Lawton Constitution,* January 15, 1953; A. E. Janzen, "Tribute to Missionary Abraham J. Becker," Message delivered at the memorial service, January 17, 1953, Post Oak Mission Records.

CHAPTER 13

1. Angie Debo, "Two Graves in Oklahoma," *Harper's Magazine,* Vol. 213, No. 1279 (December, 1956): 66.
2. A. E. Janzen to Sen. Robert S. Kerr, June 14, 1955, Post Oak Mission Records, Board of Foreign Missions, Center for Mennonite Brethren Studies, Fresno, California.
3. Report of Visit to Post Oak Mission, October 1 to 4, 1954, Post Oak Mission Records.
4. *Ibid.*
5. Report of Mr. and Mrs. H. J. Neufeld, July-September, 1955, Post Oak Mission Records; Dan Petker, Personal interview, November 12, 1995.
6. Bro. Jim and Members of Post Oak Mission to A. E. Janzen, May 1, 1955, Post Oak Mission Records.
7. H. J. Neufeld, Report to Post Oak and Lawton View Missionary Council, July 4, 1955, Post Oak Mission Records.
8. A. E. Janzen, Unpublished autobiography, Center for Mennonite Brethren Studies, Hillsboro, Kansas, 414.
9. Janzen to Col. Dave Helms, Corps of Engineers, U. S. Army, May 31, 1956, Post Oak Mission Records.
10. Written statement of the Becker families, May 19, 1956, Post Oak Mission Records.
11. Janzen, Memorandum of the Mass Meeting, May 25, 1956, Post Oak Mission Records.
12. Memorandum, Post Oak Re-Location, September 15, 1956; Janzen to Office of Indian Affairs, Anadarko, September 19, 1956; Memorandum of the Anadarko Meeting, September 22, 1956, Post Oak Mission Records.
13. J. Lee Hogue Jr. to A. E. Janzen, June 29, 1956, Post Oak Mission Records.
14. Janzen to David A. Helms, Army Corps of Engineers, September 17, 1956, Post Oak Mission Records.
15. Janzen to Sen. Robert S. Kerr, December 28, 1956, Post Oak Mission Records.
16. Robert S. Kerr to Janzen, January 4 and January 22, 1957; John D. Bristor, Colonel, Dist. Engineer, to Janzen, January 16 and January 18, 1957, Post Oak Mission Records.

CHAPTER 14

1. Jim Arterberry, Personal interview, November 12, 1995.

2. A. E. Janzen, Memo, June, 1957, Post Oak Mission Records, Board of Foreign Missions, Center for Mennonite Brethren Studies, Fresno, California.

3. David A. Helms, Chief Real Estate Division, Corps of Engineers, to A. E. Janzen, August 26, 1958, Post Oak Mission Records.

4. William J. Becker to Janzen, July 3, 1955, Post Oak Mission Records.

5. Mayor of Lawton to Janzen, July, 1955, Post Oak Mission Records.

6. Janzen to Marvin E. Roberts, Cemetery Relocation Division, Corps of Engineers, US Army, Tulsa, Oklahoma, February 28, 1957, Post Oak Mission Records.

7. *Lawton Constitution,* June 3, 1957.

8. *Ibid.,* June 26, 1957.

9. *Ibid.,* July 10, 1957.

10. *Lawton Morning Press,* July 13, 1957; *Oklahoma City Times,* July 12, 1957.

11. *Oklahoma City Times,* July 12, 1957.

12. Barbara Goodin, Compiler, *Relocation of Post Oak Mission Cemetery* (Lawton, Oklahoma: np, 1993).

13. Glenn Becker, Personal interview, November 11, 1995; T. L. Craig and Anne Powell, "Missionary's Sons Still Serve Their Indian Neighbors," *American Funeral Director* (March, 1968): 42-45; *Lawton Constitution,* August 9 and 11, 1957; Herwanna Becker Barnard, "Comanches Cry, Too," *Prairie Lore* (October, 1978): 82. On October 2, 1965 the remains of Topsannah, or Prairie Flower, little sister of Quanah, were reburied beside the grave of her mother, Cynthia Ann Parker. The child had been two years old when "rescued" with her mother by Texas Rangers in 1860, but died three years later. The disinterment was from Asbury Cemetery near Ben Wheeler, Texas. The Becker Funeral Home assisted with the reburial service. Margaret Schmidt Hacker, *Cynthia Ann Parker: The Life and the Legend* (El Paso, Texas: Texas Western Press, 1990), 35, 40; *Lawton Constitution,* October 3, 1965.

14. A. E. Janzen, Unpublished autobiography, Center for Mennonite Brethren Studies, Hillsboro, Kansas, 417.

15. Dan Petker, Personal interview, November 12, 1995.

16. Walter Friesen to Board of Foreign Missions, April 7, 1958, Post Oak Mission Records.

17. *Ibid.,* January 14, 1958.

18. D. J. Gerbrandt, Letter to author, October 10, 1995; Jacquetta Parker McClung, Comments made at the centennial observance of Post Oak Mission, November 11, 1995, Indiahoma, Oklahoma.

19. Post Oak M. B. Church Bulletin, March 23, 1958, Post Oak Mission Records.

20. *Christian Leader,* September 16, 1986.

21. Friesen to Mission Board, January 14, 1958, Post Oak Mission Records; Minutes of the Board of Foreign Missions, March, 1958, MB Missions/Services, Box 1, Center for Mennonite Brethren Studies, Fresno, California.

CHAPTER 15

1. John A. Toews, *A History of the Mennonite Brethren Church* (Hillsboro, Kansas: Mennonite Brethren Publishing House, 1975), 212-213.

2. William T. Hagan, *United States-Comanche Relations: The Reservation Years* (1976; reprint,Norman: University of Oklahoma Press, 1990), 294.

3. This survey was done by D. J. Gerbrandt and published in the *Indian Messenger,* November, 1953.

4. John Preston Dane, "A History of Baptist Missions Among the Plains Indians of Oklahoma" (Ph.D. diss., Central Baptist Theological Seminary, Kansas City, Kansas, 1955),

200; Rhoda Asenap Tate, "Post Oak Church of Indiahoma, Oklahoma," in *Comanche County History* (Dallas: Curtis Media Corporation, 1985), 144-145.

5. A. J. Becker to H. W. Lohrenz, March 20, 1939, Post Oak Mission Records, Board of Foreign Missions, Center for Mennonite Brethren Studies, Fresno, California; Dane, "A History of Baptist Missions," 211.

6. J. B. Toews, *Pilgrimage of Faith: The Mennonite Brethren Church 1860-1990* (Winnipeg, Manitoba: Kindred Press, 1993), 92.

7. J. B. Toews, Letter to author, October 9, 1995.

8. Walter Gomez, Letter to author, April 25, 1995.

9. Quoted in Bill Neeley, *The Last Comanche Chief: The Life and Times of Quanah Parker* (New York: John Wiley & Sons, Inc., 1995), 169.

10. Minutes of the General Conference of the Mennonite Brethren Church, 1909, trans. and edited by R. C. Seibel, Center for Mennonite Brethren Studies, Hillsboro, Kansas.

11. Katie Funk Wiebe, "Who, Us, Racist?" *Christian Leader*, (January, 1996), 10.

12. The Mennonite Brethren Church expanded its ministry to Latino people in the latter 1930s by establishing several small missions in the Rio Grande Valley of South Texas. This proved to be a struggling enterprize. The Lawton View Mission became an independent Mennonite Brethren Church and a member of the Southern District Conference in 1963. Orlando Harms, *Conference in Pilgrimage* (Hillsboro, Kansas: Center for Mennonite Brethren Studies, 1992), 86-97, 230.

13. Tate, "Post Oak Church of Indiahoma, Oklahoma," 145.

14. Obituary of Maddische, Post Oak File, Center for Mennonite Brethren Studies, Hillsboro, Kansas.

15. D. J. Gerbrandt, Letter to author, October 10, 1995.

16. Following the house fire the Gomezes lived in the Parker Star House for a period of time.

17. Marjorie Gerbrandt Wiens, Comments made at the Post Oak Mission centennial observance, November 11, 1995, Indiahoma, Oklahoma.

18. Using the existence of local ongoing church congregations as the basis for judging the success of missions was suggested in Wilbert R. Shenk, "Mission and Service and the Globalization of North American Mennonites," *The Mennonite Quarterly Review* (January, 1996): 22.

EPILOGUE

1. Marjorie Koweno Kelley, Letter to author, January 3, 1996.

Bibliography

MANUSCRIPT MATERIALS

National Archives, Record Group 75, Washington D. C.
    Letter Books of the Office of Indian Affairs
Oklahoma Historical Society, Oklahoma City, OK.
    Indian-Pioneer Papers
    Kiowa Agency Files
    Letters Received by the Office of Indian Affairs (Microfilm)
    Picture Collections
Carl Albert Congressional Research and Studies Center, University of Oklahoma, Norman, OK.
    Robert S. Kerr Collection
Center for Mennonite Brethren Studies, Fresno, CA
    Post Oak Mission Records, Board of Foreign Missions, General Conference of Mennonite Brethren Churches
    Minutes of the Board of Foreign Missions, General Conference of Mennonite Brethren Churches
Center for Mennonite Brethren Studies, Hillsboro, KS
    Clerk's Record, School District No.11, Marion County, Kansas
    Minutes of the General Conference of the Mennonite Brethren Churches
    Post Oak Mission Files
Glenn Becker Collection, Lawton, OK
    A. J. and Magdalena Becker Papers and Pictures
Sam and Elsie Becker Collection, Oklahoma City, OK
    A. J. and Magdalena Becker Papers and Pictures
Museum of the Great Plains, Lawton, OK
    Post Oak Mission Collection
Post Oak Mennonite Brethren Church, Indiahoma, OK
    Church Roll and Record Books
Western History Collections, University of Oklahoma Archives, Norman, OK
    Picture Collection

DOCUMENTS OF THE UNITED STATES GOVERNMENT

Senate. Subcommittee of Indian Affairs. Survey of the Condition of Indians in the U. S., 71st Cong., 33rd sess., November 17-22, 1930. Washington D. C.: U. S. Printing Office, 1931.

United States Department of the Interior. Annual Report of the Board of Indian Commissioners for the Year Ended June 30, 1932. Washington D. C.: U. S. Printing Office, 1932.

BOOKS

Bekker, Jacob P. *Origin of the Mennonite Brethren Church*, trans. D. E. Pauls and A. E. Janzen. Hillsboro, KS: Mennonite Brethren Publishing House, 1973.

Berkhover, Robert E. Jr. *Salvation and the Savage, An Analysis of Protestant Missions and the American Indian Response, 1787-1862.* Lexington: University of Kentucky Press, 1965.

Berthrong, Donald J. *The American Indian: From Pacifism to Activism.* Saint Louis: Forum Press, 1973.

____. *The Cheyenne and Arapaho Ordeal.* Norman: University of Oklahoma Press, 1976.

Clark, Blue. *Lone Wolf v Hitchcock: Treaty Rights and Indian Law at the End of the Nineteenth Century.* Lincoln: University of Nebraska Press, 1994.

Comanche County History. Dallas: Curtis Media Corporation, 1985.

Ellis, Clyde. *To Change Them Forever: Indian Education at the Rainy Mountain Boarding School, 1893-1920.* Norman: University of Oklahoma Press, 1996.

Epp, Margaret A. *No Hand Sam and Other Missionary Stories.* Hillsboro, KS: Mennonite Brethren Publishing House, 1959.

Esau, Mrs. H. T. *First Sixty Years of M. B. Missions.* Hillsboro, KS: Mennonite Brethren Publishing House, 1954.

Gibson, Arrell M. *The American Indian: Prehistory to the Present.* Lexington: D. C. Heath and Co., 1980.

Goodin, Barbara, comp. *Relocation of Post Oak Mission Cemetery.* Lawton: n.p., 1933.

Hacker, Margaret Schmidt. *Cynthia Ann Parker: The Life and the Legend.* El Paso, TX: Texas Western Press, 1990.

Hagan, William T. *Quanah Parker, Comanche Chief.* Norman: University of Oklahoma Press, 1993.

____. *United States-Comanche Relations: The Reservation Years.* 1976; reprint, Norman: University of Oklahoma Press, 1990.

Harms, J. F. *Geschichte der Mennoniten Brüdergemeinde, 1860-1924.* Hillsboro, KS: Mennonite Brethren Publishing House, 1924.

Harms, Orlando. *Conference in Pilgrimage.* Hillsboro, KS: Center for Mennonite Brethren Studies, 1992.

Janzen, A. E. *Foreign Missions.* Hillsboro, KS: Board of Foreign Missions, 1946.

Jones, David E. *Sanapia: Comanche Medicine Woman.* Prospect Heights, IL: Waveland Press, Inc., 1984.

Kappler, Charles J. *Indian Laws and Treaties,* II. Washington, D.C.: Government Printing Office, 1903-27.

Kavanagh, Thomas W. *Comanche Political History: An Ethnohistorical Perspective 1706-1875.* Lincoln: University of Nebraska Press, 1996.

Krehbiel, H. P. *History of the Mennonite General Conference,* I. Saint Louis: A. Weibusch and Son Printing Co., 1898.

Kroeker, Marvin E. *Great Plains Command: William B. Hazen in the Frontier West.* Norman: University of Oklahoma Press, 1976.

Leckie, William H. *The Military Conquest of the Southern Plains.* Norman: University of Oklahoma Press, 1963.

Lohrenz, John H. *The Mennonite Brethren Church.* Hillsboro, KS: Mennonite Brethren Publishing House, 1950.

Milner, Clyde A. II and O'Neil, Floyd A., eds., *Churchmen and the Western Indians, 1820-1920.* Norman: University of Oklahoma Press, 1985.

Neeley, Bill. *The Last Comanche Chief: The Life and Times of Quanah Parker.* New York: John Wiley & Sons, Inc. 1995.

Nye, W. S. *Carbine and Lance.* Norman: University of Oklahoma Press, 1943.

Parman, Don. *Indians and the American West in the Twentieth Century.* Bloomington: Indiana University Press, 1994.

Peters, Gerhard W. *The Growth of Foreign Missions in the Mennonite Brethren Church.* Hillsboro, KS: The Board of Foreign Missions, 1952.

____. *Foundations of Mennonite Brethren Missions.* Hillsboro, KS: Kindred Press, 1984.

Post Oak Mission Centennial. Oklahoma City: Taylor Publishing Co., 1995.

Prucha, Francis Paul. *American Indian Policy in the Formative Years.* Cambridge: Harvard University Press, 1962.

____. *The Churches and the Indian Schools, 1888-1912.* Lincoln: University of Nebraska Press, 1979.

Ratzlaff, ElRoy. *God's Call to Mexico: The Story of Rev. Walter Gomez, Founder of MMM.* Pharr, TX: Mexican Mission Ministries, Inc., 1994

Richardson, R. N. *The Comanche Barrier to South Plains Settlement.* Glendale: Arthur H. Clark, 1933.

Stewart, Omer C. *Peyote Religion.* Norman: University of Oklahoma Press, 1987.

Szasz, Margaret Connell. *Education and the American Indian.* Albuquerque: University of New Mexico Press, 1974.

Tidwell, Clara Sue. *Choctaws and Missionaries in Mississippi, 1818- 1918.* Norman: University of Oklahoma Press, 1995.

Toews, John A. *A History of the Mennonite Brethren Church.* Hillsboro, KS: Mennonite Brethren Publishing House, 1975.

Toews, J. B. *Pilgrimage of Faith: The Mennonite Brethren Church 1860-1990.* Winnipeg, MB: Kindred Press, 1993.

Tyler, S. Lyman. *A History of Indian Policy.* Washington, D. C.: United States Department of the Interior, 1973.

Utley, Robert and Washburn, Wilcomb. *Indian Wars.* New York:Houghton Mifflin Co., 1985.

Wallace, Ernest and Hoebel, E. Adamson. *The Comanches: Lords of the South Plains.* Norman: University of Oklahoma Press, 1952.

Wiebe, Katie, ed. *Women among the Brethren.* Hillsboro, KS: Board of Christian Literature of the General Conference of the Mennonite Brethren Church, 1979.

ARTICLES

Barnard, Herwanna Becker. "Comanches Cry, Too." *Prairie Lore* (October, 1978).

Becker, A. J. "Biography of Mrs. Magdalena Hergert Becker." *Christmas Greetings* (December, 1942).

___. "The Story of Post Oak." *Zionsbote* (November 28, 1945).

Becker, Daniel A. "Comanche Civilization, with History of Quanah Parker." *Chronicles of Oklahoma,* I, No. 3 (June, 1923).

Becker, W. J. "The Comanche Indian and His Language." *Chronicles of Oklahoma,* XIV, No. 3 (September, 1936).

Brown, Opal Hartsell. "Russian Refugee—Missionary to the Indians." *Prairie Lore* (April, 1979).

Corwin, Hugh D. "Protestant Missionary Work among the Comanches and Kiowas." *Chronicles of Oklahoma,* 46 (Spring, 1968).

Craig, T. L. and Powell, Anne. "Missionary's Sons Still Serve Their Neighbors." *American Funeral Director* (March, 1968).

Dalke, Herbert M. "Seventy-five Years of Missions in Oklahoma." *Mennonite Life* (July, 1955).

Debo, Angie. "Two Graves in Oklahoma." *Harper's Magazine,* Vol. 213, No. 1279 (December, 1956).

Dyck, Stanley P. "The Halstead Indian Industrial School." *Mennonite Life* (June, 1987).

Haley, J. Evetts. "The Last Great Chief." *The Shamrock* (Spring, 1957).

Harper, Richard H. "The Missionary Work of the Reformed (Dutch) Church in America in Oklahoma." *Chronicles of Oklahoma,* XVIII, No. 4 (December, 1940).

Herring, Rebecca. "Their Work Was Never Done: Women Missionaries on the Kiowa-Comanche Reservation." *Chronicles of Oklahoma,* 64 (Spring, 1986).

Hume, C. Ross. "Pioneer Missionary Enterprises of Kiowa, Comanche, and Wichita Indian Reservation." *Chronicles of Oklahoma,* XXXIX, No.1(Spring, 1951).

Juhnke, James C. "General Conference Mennonite Missions to the American Indians in the Late Nineteenth Century." *Mennonite Quarterly Review* (April, 1980).

Kohfeld, Henry. "Meine Erfahrungen von der Liebe und Treue Gottes." *Zionsbote* (July 10, 17, 24, 31, 1929).

Kroeker, Marvin E. "Die Stillen im Lande: Mennonites in the Oklahoma Land Rushes." *Chronicles of Oklahoma,* LXVII, No.1(Spring, 1989).

Monahan, Forrest D., Jr. "The Kiowa-Comanche Reservation in the 1890's." *Chronicles of Oklahoma,* XLV, No. 4 (Winter, 1967-1968).

Shenk, Wilbert R. "Mission and Service and the Globalization of North American Mennonites." *Mennonite Quarterly Review* (January, 1996).

Vernon, Walter N. "Methodist Beginnings Among Southwest Oklahoma Indians." *Chronicles of Oklahoma,* LVIII, No. 4 (Winter, 1980-1981).

Wiebe, Katie Funk. "Who, Us, Racist?" *Christian Leader* (January, 1966).

UNPUBLISHED MANUSCRIPTS, THESES, AND DISSERTATIONS

Barnard, Herwanna Becker. "The Comanche and His Literature, with an Anthology of His Myths, Legends, Folktales, Oratory, Poetry, and Songs." M. A. Thesis, University of Oklahoma, 1941.

Becker, William J. "The Compounding of Words in the Comanche Indian Language." M. A. Thesis, University of Oklahoma, 1931.

Dane, John Preston. "A History of Baptist Missions Among the Plains Indians of Oklahoma." Ph. D. Dissertation, Central Baptist Theological Seminary, Kansas City, Kansas, 1955.

Emmerich, Lisa E. "'To Respect and Love and Seek the Ways of White Women': Field Matrons, the Office of Indian Affairs, and Civilization Policy, 1890-1938." Ph. D. Dissertation, University of Maryland, 1987.

Herring, Rebecca Jane. "Failed Assimilation: Anglo Women on the Kiowa-Comanche Reservation, 1867-1906." M. A. Thesis, Texas Tech University, 1983.

Janzen, A. E. *Autobiography.* typed manuscript, Center For Mennonite Brethren Studies, Hillsboro, KS.

Peters, David Charles, ed. *Kudrich oba Lustig: Edited Writings of David Cornelius Peters (1883-1975).* Unpublished manuscript, Center for Mennonite Brethren Studies, Hillboro, KS.

NEWSPAPERS

Cache Register, 1911.
Christian Leader, 1950-1996.
Daily Oklahoman, 1911, 1930.
Lawton Constitution, 1930, 1938, 1953, 1957, 1963, 1965.
Lawton Morning Press, 1957.
Lawton News Review, 1930.
Oklahoma City Times, 1957.
The Indian Messenger, 1948, 1953-1954.
Washita County Enterprise, 1974.
Zionsbote, 1899-1929.

INTERVIEWS

Arterberry, Jim. Interview with author, November 12, 1995.

Becker, A. J. Interview with Sam Becker, December 25, 1948 (Tape).

Becker, Elsie. Interview with author, October 17, 1996.

Becker, Glenn. Interview with author, May 1, 1994, March 20, August 13, November 11, 1995.

Gordon, Edith Kassanavoid. Interview with author, November 12, 1995.

Hoahwah, Carleton. Interview with author, March 19, 1995.

Kelley, Marjorie Koweno. Interview with author, August 6, November 11, 1995.

Kohfeld, Henry, Jr. Interview with author, May 27, 1994.

Maddox, Mary Alice. Interview with author, August 6, 1995.

Pahcheka, Lizzie. Interview with author, August 6, 1995.

Petker, Dan. Interview with author, November 12, 1995.

Wiens, Marjorie Gerbrandt. Interview with author, November 11, 1995.

Woesner, Herbert. Interview with author, March 18, 1996.

LETTERS

Gerbrandt, Dick J. Letter to author, October 10, 1995.

Gomez, Walter. Letter to author, April 25, 1995.

Kelley, Marjorie Koweno. Letter to author, January 3, 1996.

Toews, J. B. Letter to author, October 9, 1995.

Index

Symbols

4-H Club 85

A

Adrian, Cycil 147
agriculture. *See farmers*
Allotment Policy 84
American Baptists
   2, 3, 18, 35, 71–72
American Mennonite Brethren
   Mission Union 45
Anadarko Indian School 46
Anadarko, Oklahoma
   13, 26, 46, 53, 71, 80, 123, 150
Apaches 7–8, 14
Arapahos 2, 72
Arterberry family 147
Asenap, Arlene 42, 153
Asenap, Herman (Greyfoot) 39, 42-
   43, 49, 60, 76, 97, 105, 117, 133–
   134, 141, 144, 153
Asenap, Rowena 89

B

Baldwin, Major Frank 13
Banks, Lena 90
Barnard, Herwanna Becker
   20, 41, 62, 132, 152–155,
   161, 165–166
Bartel, Harry 107–108
Becker, Abraham Jacob: appointed
   head missionary 35; as assistant to
   Kohfeld 25–29; attends
   McPherson College 25; camp
   meetings as mission strategy, 73–
   74; conducts funeral service for
   Quanah Parker, 60–61; conducts
   reburial service for Cynthia Ann

Parker, 58; death, 117; death of
   wife, 96–98; on establishing
   mission school, 109; expansion of
   activities, 86; expansion of
   Mexican ministry, 93–95; as
   featured speaker at dedication of
   Parker monument, 89; fights to
   save Post Oak from confiscation,
   114–115; first baptisms by, 40;
   helps construct buildings at Post
   Oak Mission, x; home visitation
   ministry, 50; homesteads in
   Cherokee Outlet, x; marriage to
   Magdalena Hergert, 25; missionary
   work evaluated, 137–145;
   organization of Comanche
   Mennonite Brethren congregation,
   44; reburies Quanah's bones, 62;
   reliance on interpreters, 43;
   remarriage, 103; resigns from
   Mexican work, 107; retirement
   from Post Oak, 102; supervises
   Lawton Mexican work, 103, 106–
   107; takes steps towards ending
   mission status of Post Oak, 101;
   tent meeting, Red Store, 39–40;
   visits to churches, 69–70
Becker, Augusta 30
Becker, Daniel 59, 80
Becker Funeral Home
   64, 105, 116, 131, 161
Becker, Glenn vii, 34, 58, 63–64,
   71, 77, 87-88, 95-97, 100, 113,
   116–117, 128, 132, 149, 152–
   156, 160–161, 163, 167
Becker, Herwanna 69. *See Barnard,
   Herwanna Becker*
Becker, Jacob P. 1
Becker, Magdalena Hergert: aids
   woman in paternity case, 80–81;
   appointed field matron, 30;
   concern for sick, 50–51; conver-

Civilization program 9
Clark, Alberta 89
Coffee, Pete 118, 133–134
Collier, John 109
Comanches: alliance with Kiowas, 5; burial customs, 20; capture Cynthia Ann Parker, 6; Comancheria, 6; early history, 3–5; impact of the Great Depression, 84–85, 93; induct Gerbrandts into Quahada band, 110; major bands, 45; missions among, 45; number in farming, 93; population figures, 45, 92, 138–139; Quahada resistance to Christianity, 28; treaties with U.S., 7–8; tribal cemetery authorized near Cache, 129
Cook Christian Training School 147
Corn Bible Academy 106, 140
Corn Mennonite Brethren Church 97, 98
Corn, Oklahoma 2, 18, 95, 97, 105–107, 123, 159
Cox, Emmet 59
Curtis, Representative Charles 14, 151

D

Dalmeny, Saskatchewan, Canada 44
deaconesses 21
Dean, Anona Birdsong 142
"Death House" 51–52
Decoration Day 57, 63, 85, 113
Department of Defense 114, 124
Deyo, Anna 30, 34, 152–154
Deyo, Elton Cyrus 3, 35, 37, 46, 59–60, 72, 140
Deyo Mission 37, 45, 47, 73, 79, 131
Dick, John S. 101
Dick, Tina 103, 105

Dick, Wilma 105, 159
District farmers 46. *See also farmers*
Driscoll, Louise 78, 156
Dutch Reformed Mission 11, 45, 72, 151

E

Ebenezer Mennonite Brethren Church 21
Ebenfeld Mennonite Brethren Church 21
Edmond, Oklahoma 117
Elk Creek 2–3
Emmerich, Lisa E. 154, 157–158 166

F

Fairview, Oklahoma 18, 25, 26, 66, 70, 72, 107, 127
Farm Women's Club 85
farmers 7, 9, 26, 46, 48, 54, 84, 116, 124
farming. *See farmers*
Fast, Clarence 145
Fast, Edna 105
Fast, J.W. 127
field matrons iii, 31, 46, 52–53, 65, 72, 77, 80, 84, 91, 154, 157–158, 166
Field, Vernon 129
Figueroa family 147
First Baptist Church, Lawton 117
First Comanche Mission. *See Deyo Mission*
Five Civilized Tribes 7
Fort Parker 6
Fort Sill 3, 8, 11, 1314, 17, 23, 46, 57, 67, 85, 89, 111, 114-115, 119, 122, 128–132
Fort Sill Indian Hospital 46